CREATING A HABITAT FOR HUMANITY

"Jonathan Reckford has captured the spirit of Habitat for Humanity with stories and experiences that tell the true meaning of 'love thy neighbor as thyself.' This book is an encouragement for all people to join forces and build homes, eliminating poverty housing and building stronger communities."

—Janet Huckabee, First Lady of Arkansas and coordinator for Governor's Wives Women Build Program

"An inspiring look at an inspirational organization . . . .Habitat's new CEO has clearly embraced the mission, vision and values of his organization. By telling heartfelt stories, referencing biblical passages, and asking readers to reflect on their own purpose in life, Reckford builds a powerful case for how we can eliminate substandard housing in our lifetime."

—Bruce Nicholson, President and CEO, Thrivent Financial for Lutherans

"Consistently asking readers what role they will play in the global problem of homelessness, Reckford prods individuals, congregations, and groups to get personally involved in the struggle, rather than simply donating money from their armchairs. . . . Reckford's passion for, and commitment to, his cause is clear and persuasive."
    —*Publisher's Weekly*

"Reckford's account of Habitat for Humanity's contribution to the realization of the Millennium Development Goals is truly inspiring. The book should stir civil society organizations to scale up their efforts and hold governments accountable to meet their commitment to achieve the Millennium Goals. The Right to Shelter along with the other Millennium Goals are indeed basic human rights."
    —Salil Shetty, Director, United Nations Millennium Campaign

"Thank you, Jonathan Reckford, for elevating our sights beyond today's polarizing political and religious polemics and so inspiringly reminding us that there is no higher calling than the common ground of serving 'the least of these.'"
    —Neal Keny-Guyer, CEO, Mercy Corps

"Jonathan Reckford draws from his rich experience to offer us a thoughtful perspective on how we Christians and non-Christians alike may engage with the issues of housing for the poor. His discussion is both informative and stirring. He gives us beautiful stories of individuals finding hope, communities coming together and God working through the obedient to show justice and mercy. As he explores the full dimensions of God's commandments in Micah 6:8, I am struck by how much the world needs justice and mercy today, and what a joy it is to pursue these and take part in sharing God's Kingdom."
    —Dean R. Hirsch, President, World Vision International

CREATING A
HABITAT FOR
HUMANITY

No Hands but Yours

Jonathan T. M. Reckford

Foreword by Jimmy Carter

Fortress Press
Minneapolis

CREATING A HABITAT FOR HUMANITY
No Hands but Yours

Cover and interior images: Courtesy of Habitat for Humanity
Cover design: Kevin van der Leek Design Inc.
Book design: Jessica A. Puckett

Library of Congress Cataloging-in-Publication Data

Reckford, Jonathan T. M., 1962-
  Creating a habitat for humanity : no hands but yours / Jonathan T. M. Reckford;
foreword by Jimmy Carter.
     p. cm.
  Includes bibliographical references.
  ISBN 978-0-8006-3888-7 (alk. paper)
  1. Church work with the homeless. 2. Church work with the poor. 3. Housing—
Religious aspects—Christianity. 4. Habitat for Humanity International, Inc. I.
Title.
BV4456.R43 2007
261.8'325--dc22   2006038918

Contents

Jimmy and Rosalynn Carter work on the construction of a house at the Jimmy Carter Work Project 2003.

FOREWORD

When I wrote the book *Talking Peace: A Vision for the Next Generation*, I devoted a substantial chapter to the "three basic building blocks of peace": food, shelter, and health care. While that may have surprised readers looking only to learn about the high-profile Camp David Accords or the Carter Center's worldwide mediation efforts, any discussion of the search for peace without acknowledging those three important physical needs ultimately would be meaningless.

Through the Carter Center, Rosalynn and I have been privileged to work with experts in improving agricultural production and heath care in many of the world's poorest countries. Through our work with Habitat for Humanity, we have had the opportunity to build houses and to shine a spotlight on the desperate need for decent, affordable shelter. These aren't just activities to fill our days; they are among the ways we choose to wage peace.

Habitat for Humanity is a remarkable organization filled with stories of hope and joy, physical exertion, and aching muscles. In *No Hands but Yours*, Habitat Chief Executive Officer Jonathan Reckford looks at housing through the lenses of mercy, humility, and justice, and invites readers to evaluate their own response to the immense need for secure shelter.

It has been said that most people take their homes for granted, but that no one who has been homeless or who has worked on a Habitat house ever does. This is a book that will put serious readers in the same category. Whether you are reading as an individual or as part of a study group, it's unlikely you will ever view housing quite the same way again.

Housing as mercy, humility, justice, a foundation for peace—decent shelter can be viewed as all of these. Rosalynn and I have been blessed to be able to make a small difference through an organization with a big mission: a world where everyone has an acceptable place to live, where creating and maintaining a habitat for humanity becomes everyone's goal.

—*Former U.S. President Jimmy Carter*

INTRODUCTION

"¿*Por que está aqui?*" "Why are you here?"

The question came to me from a lovely fifteen-year-old girl named Haylim as we worked alongside one another building a home for her and her mother in the village of Amecameca, outside Mexico City. They had been sharing a two-room house with another family of five and were within weeks of having their own home. I had answered that question many times conceptually, of course. But it was different trying to explain to a young girl why strangers from around the world and around Mexico were there to help her family realize their dream.

I told Haylim that I was there for three reasons: First, because I believe that we are all one in God's eyes and that God cares passionately for every single person in the world. Second, because I believe that everyone should have the opportunity to live in a safe, decent, affordable home. And third, because every time I have the privilege of working alongside someone like her, it gives me a glimpse of the kind of person I aspire to be and the kind of community we are called to create.

That's also why I am writing this book. Because housing matters. Lives are at stake. I joined Habitat for Humanity a year ago, and both the desperate need for decent, affordable homes around the world and the remarkable ways God continues to work through this ministry to change lives have powerfully affected my life. I hope this book will introduce the reader to the need for affordable housing and, more than that, will issue a personal call to become part of the solution. I also hope it will give people a greater understanding of what we have learned in thirty years of service at Habitat for Humanity and how we are evolving to address the need for decent housing. There are many ways to address housing, and I hope these reflections will spark creative ideas in you for doing so. Our mission is not just about building houses, as critically important as those homes are. Our mission is to transform communities.

As I reflect on that experience with Haylim and so many like it, I realize that it parallels my "life verse" from the Bible:

> *He has showed you, O man, what is good.*
> *And what does the* Lord *require of you?*
> *To act justly and to love mercy*
> *and to walk humbly with your God.*
> *(Micah 6:6–8)*

This has been a familiar passage all my life, though one that has taken on more meaning for me over time. My grandmother, Millicent Fenwick, was a towering figure in my childhood. A civil- and human-rights pioneer as well as New Jersey congresswoman, she used to recite it to me every time I saw her. She had an imposing presence. Prior to her public life, she had written the best-selling *Vogue Book of Etiquette* (a million copies sold in 1948), so in order to graduate to the "grown-up" table at her house, one had to be able to sit up straight, hold one's fork properly, and participate in discussions of food problems in sub-Saharan Africa. At some point in every visit, she would quote Micah, which is as applicable to Habitat's mission as it is to each of our lives. So that's all we have to do. Act justly, love mercy, and walk humbly with our God.

I chose that verse to be the organizing structure for this book because it is helpful to see poverty housing through the lenses of justice, mercy, and humility—three desperate needs in our world. I'm taking the liberty of following that structure in the way I explained it to Haylim.

Ending poverty housing is a matter of mercy or compassion. As we are so blessed, we are called to be a blessing.

The imperative for compassion cries out to each and every one of us. For religious persons, it is perhaps even more keenly articulated. Bob Pierce, the founder of World Vision, wrote these words as he witnessed the suffering of children and poor people during the Korean War: "Let my heart be broken with the things that break the heart of God." Our challenge is to deliver a similar call to action. Chapter 1 calls us to find the current state of poverty housing in our world unacceptable, and Chapter 2 calls us to respond to that discontent in community. Decent houses meet a critical physical need and are part of a greater need for relationship and sustainable communities. As we are the beneficiaries of God's unmerited grace, how do we then become the hands and feet of Jesus in the world? We need to focus both on the end and the means of achieving our goal.

Ending poverty housing is a matter of justice. We believe everyone deserves the opportunity to live in a decent, affordable home.

Justice, too, is a universal imperative, perhaps nowhere more compellingly announced than in the teachings of Jesus. If we take Jesus' teaching seriously, it is clear that we have a duty to be kingdom builders—to do whatever we can to mold our world in God's image and to bring hope, to create God's "habitat for humanity." If we were designing a system for a just society, in which each person had a proportionate chance of ending up in any socioeconomic stratum, it is unlikely we would create a world with such an unconscionable gap between the haves and have-nots. Part Two of this book lays out the staggering need for affordable housing in the United States and around the world and shows the transforming role of decent shelter in helping break the cycle of poverty, affecting health and education for children and providing a foundation for a better life.

Ending poverty housing is a matter of humility. The universal experience of participants with Habitat and other such programs is that we receive more than we give.

Randall Wallace, the screenwriter of *Braveheart* (among other films), says it succinctly: "Habitat for Humanity is a perpetual motion miracle. Everyone who receives, gives—and everyone who gives, receives. If you want to live complacent and uninspired, stay away from Habitat. Come close to Habitat and it will change you and make you part of something that changes the world."

One of the joys of my work is getting to see so many families whose lives are transformed. A crucial aspect of the way Habitat works is that the transformation takes place just as much in the lives of the volunteers as in the lives of the home owners. Chapter 5 demonstrates how the process of bringing people together from different races, faiths, and socioeconomic backgrounds for the very tangible act of creating or improving a home breaks down barriers and opens hearts.

Another favorite piece of wisdom of mine comes from theologian and author Henry Blackaby, who says that if you're not sure what to do, look for where God is at work and join him there. I see God's hands clearly at work in the Habitat movement and am privileged to participate. Habitat for Humanity's ultimate goal is an audacious one: to eliminate poverty housing and homelessness from the face of the earth by building adequate and basic housing. Furthermore, all our words and actions are for the ultimate purpose of putting shelter on the hearts and minds of people in such a powerful way that poverty housing and homelessness become socially, politically, and religiously unacceptable.

While our tactics continuously evolve, we adhere relentlessly to six core principles that guide how we work. We aim to:

1. demonstrate the love and teachings of Jesus Christ
2. advocate on behalf of those in need of decent shelter
3. focus on shelter by building and renovating simple, decent, affordable houses
4. engage broad community through inclusive leadership and diverse partnerships
5. promote dignity through full partnership with Habitat home owners and future home partners
6. promote transformational and sustainable community development.

It is important to note that I am writing from my perspective as a follower of Jesus. Habitat for Humanity is an ecumenical Christian ministry. We are motivated by Christ's call to serve and love our neighbors. We are inclusive and nondiscriminatory. We joyfully welcome people of any faith or no faith to join in our mission to eradicate poverty. Regardless of your particular faith perspective, there is a universal moral imperative to change the conditions that have so many in our world living in such desperate conditions. I hope this book will spur you to be part of the solution.

So as you read this book, think about the question: *¿Por qué está aquí?* Why are you here? Chapter 6 enumerates many ways that you can make a difference in the battle to eliminate poverty housing from the face of the earth and personally to experience authentic community. Come help build it!

Acknowledgments

I wish to express my gratitude to the many people who made this project possible. First of all, to Pam Campbell, my collaborator and editor, without whom the book would never have happened. Her research, attention to detail, patience with my schedule and ability to bring form to my musings and ideas made this possible. To Jill Claflin and Jennifer Lindsey, whose wisdom helped structure the book and keep it focused. To Michael West and the team at Fortress Press for their support and faith in the project. To the staff, volunteers and homeowner partners of Habitat for Humanity, who provide the stories and inspiration for the book and demonstrate daily what community can look like. I'd like to thank you personally for purchasing this book. All royalties will go to support our mission, which is what this is all about.

Any finally, this book is dedicated to my wife, Ashley, my partner in life and ministry, for sharing this adventure with me.

PART ONE
HOUSING
AND MERCY

Christ has no body now but yours,
No hands but yours,
No feet but yours.
Yours are the eyes through which
Christ's compassion must look out on the world,
Yours are the feet with which
He is to go about doing good.
Yours are the hands with which
He is to bless us now.

—St. Teresa of Avila

Somwang Chiochan, a Habitat home owner in Thachatchai, Thailand, has been given the official title of "tsunami watcher." His house is built higher than the others in the community so he can keep an eye on the ocean in case another tsunami comes.

CHAPTER 1
CALLED TO CARE

During a visit to the tsunami-devastated countries in 2005, I encountered a developmentally disabled gentleman named Somwang Chiochan, who lived in a village of Moken, or sea gypsies, near Phuket, Thailand. The Moken people are discriminated against; and because of his disability, Mr. Chiochan was further discriminated against by the Moken people. Before the calamity, he held no role in the fishing village, and he lived humbly on a 2 x 3 square-meter lot in a structure that was worse than most doghouses. You might say he embodied "the least of these brothers and sisters of Christ," at least as measured in material possessions and social status.

As the people of the community began rebuilding after the storm, however, transformation happened in a number of ways. The elders of the village decided that it was not acceptable for Mr. Chiochan to live in those conditions any longer. They didn't have any more land, so their solution was to build the village's first and only three-story watchtower. For the first time, Mr. Chiochan has a safe, decent home—with the best view in town. In addition, the elders gave him the job of being the watchman for the village to monitor the sea for future storms. Now Mr. Chiochan has not only a place to live but also a place in the community.

I had the gift of dedicating that home, and Mr. Chiochan took great pride in showing it to me and telling about his task as watchman. That was indeed holy ground.

Blessed Are the Merciful

The decent thing for the community to do after the storm would have been to help Mr. Chiochan rebuild exactly the same home he lost. However, mercy called for more. God's mercy and grace often call people to radical behavior. Mercy said, "Let's give Mr. Chiochan a place of honor in the community. Let's take what we have and find a way to make it better."

While he helped build his new home, it was more house than he could have afforded or built by himself. His neighbors responded to him out of mercy and chose to give him the gifts of honor and dignity. That gesture is much like grace, God's unconditional love for us, which is not dependent upon our actions or our goodness. We don't earn grace. Grace is God's love freely given.

"Mercy" is a powerful word from Scripture that pulses throughout Habitat for Humanity. One of our mission principles is to demonstrate the love and teachings of Jesus Christ, and the tangible way we do that is by building houses in partnership with those in need of a decent, safe, and affordable place in which to live.

The Global Picture

Some 1.2 billion people worldwide live on the equivalent of less than $1 per day. Finding the simplest shelter is often a struggle. Many poor families are without transportation to get to and from a job. Feeding the family may be a priority, but sometimes there is just not enough to eat. Although education may be free, many families do not have the money for supplies or school uniforms. Medical care is often out of the question.

We cannot allow the magnitude of the problem to stop us from doing our part, however. Innovative thinking will enable us to partner with even more families in new ways, and we draw energy from hearing stories like that of Mr. Chiochan, stories that remind us of the goodness and mercy in the hearts of many people.

Mercy as Taking Action

Most often, mercy refers to acts of compassion—between individuals or between God and people. Mercy is not just a feeling. It is accompanied by an action—or a request for action. In the Scripture verse that helps shape this book, the prophet Micah says that loving mercy is one of the three things that God requires in our lives. We are to reach out to others in acts of mercy. The Gospels in the New Testament contain many references to mercy that indicate its varied meanings and point out expectations.

In the Sermon on the Mount in Matthew 5:7, Jesus says, "Blessed are the merciful, for they will be shown mercy." Those who show compassion to others, who have a caring and giving heart, will be shown compassion.

At the end of the parable of the Good Samaritan in Luke 10:36-37, Jesus asked, "Which of these three do you think was a neighbor to the man who fell into the hands of robbers?"

The expert in the law replied, "The one who had mercy on him."

Jesus told him, "Go and do likewise."

The Samaritan disregarded all manner of social and political rules because he felt called to offer assistance to the injured man. He showed mercy because compassionate response was the most important requirement of that moment. He interrupted his day and totally inconvenienced himself to care for the one in need. Theologian Henri Nouwen said we are frustrated by the interruptions in life until we realize that the interruptions are life. Jesus calls us to be neighbors by showing mercy—especially when it interrupts our day or forces us out of our comfort zones or requires us to step out in faith.

In *The Cotton Patch Version of Luke and Acts*, Clarence Jordan retells the parable of the Good Samaritan with a white preacher, a white gospel song leader, and a black man as the travelers who saw the injured man on the road. When the question arose about who acted as a neighbor, the traditional version answers, "The one who had mercy on him." *The Cotton Patch Version* says, "The one who treated me kindly." Thus, mercy is equated with the action of showing kindness.

> WE ARE FRUSTRATED BY THE INTERRUPTIONS IN LIFE UNTIL WE REALIZE THAT THE INTERRUPTIONS ARE LIFE.

Mercy as More than the Minimum

Mercy is a result of becoming personally involved. It is the difference between writing a check or dropping off a bag of used clothes and taking the time to care for others who have an immediate need. That was certainly the experience of Forest Griswold of Springfield, Oregon, who came to love the people in the Batticaloa community of Sri Lanka, where he went to offer help in 2005 following the devastating tsunami:

> I was at home watching the news, drinking coffee, and getting ready to go to work when I first heard about the tsunami. The first images I saw were of giant waves washing over people and buildings, sweeping away everything in their path. I was shocked by the enormity of the loss of life and devastation to buildings and the environment. In the face of natural disasters, the power of nature makes man and his endeavors insignificant by comparison. I thought a lot about my dad who had passed away in January of 2004 from cancer. I could really empathize with the people who had lost loved ones in the storm.

> I have always wanted to do something tangible to help people in need, but I was never really sure how to go about it. The opportunity to become part of a Habitat for Humanity team did not come until early February when Bob Bell, a long-time Habitat volunteer, became a customer of mine. He approached me about joining a team that would be going to Sri Lanka in March for some of the first rebuilding efforts. I didn't know much about Sri Lanka, but I knew it was one of the hardest

hit areas. I had never done any relief work before, but I thought about it, talked it over with my wife and decided to go.

Meeting so many people who were impacted by the disaster was so much more personal than seeing it on television. Also, it is hard to get a true sense of the magnitude of the disaster by looking at pictures or video. My job was to be a construction laborer. The tools we had to work with were very limited, and that made a lot of our work very labor intensive.

I truly did love meeting the local folks; they were so welcoming and kind to us. I will always have a special spot in my heart for the Sri Lankan people. One thing that I remember fondly is two little girls shyly approaching me as I worked. They came to shake my hand and to introduce themselves to me. There also was a little boy who was very boisterous and enjoyed talking to us in Tamil. He enjoyed playing with our tools. Sometimes they would bring a tray of sodas or juice for us to drink, or they would bring us a coconut with the end chopped off and a straw in it to allow us to drink the milk. After we drank our fill, they would take a machete and chop the coconuts open so we could eat the meat.

It was very hard to leave. A part of me would have liked to have stayed and helped more. The best part was building the relationships with the people. I hope what lasts forever is the ripple effect created by people joining together to help each other through difficult experiences.

I gained an appreciation of our commonality and that truly we are one people.

Stories like these are profoundly inspiring to me. Building houses is a good thing—and desperately needed—but just building houses wouldn't fulfill our mission of transforming people and communities. Without relationships, Habitat would have no purpose. There would be no meaningful exchange. It is always humbling to be reminded of this and to reinforce my sights on the important things in Habitat's world: God's children in need of housing and those called to help meet that need through honest partnership.

Holy Discontent

For some people the call to social action comes over time. It is a buildup of various events and circumstances that culminates at key moments. For me one of those moments was in 2002, when I was on a mission trip to India. I was working with the Bhangi Dalits, the most marginalized group in the country, who were allowed only to hand-clean latrines and to clean up after dead animals. They lived in abject poverty, desperately struggling for a better way. Without some intervention, half the children there die by the age of 13.

Seeing children living in those conditions devastated me. It is hard to describe the contrast between them and a similar group who were in school and healthy with a

> FOR SOME PEOPLE THE CALL TO SOCIAL ACTION COMES OVER TIME. IT IS A BUILDUP OF VARIOUS EVENTS AND CIRCUMSTANCES THAT CULMINATES AT KEY MOMENTS.

chance for a fundamentally different life. The futures of the schoolchildren were hopeful because God had touched the heart and hands of the founder of the Rural Presbyterian Church, whose ministry had created enterprises, schools, and training to emancipate these Dalits. It was through the children who had no champion that I felt God's presence. I felt his pull on my heart and a renewed passion for those left out in our societies.

Bill Hybels, pastor at the Willow Creek Community Church near Chicago, would call that "holy discontent," which he distinguishes from mere discontent along these lines: Discontent is when you or I watch a terrible event unfold on television, remark that something ought to be done about it, then tune in quickly to the movie of the week. Holy discontent, he says, is when you or I watch the same event and it wrecks us. It is when God seizes us so that we put down the remote control and feel an urgency to respond.

Encountering those children in India had such an effect on me that I had to take action. It wasn't that I initiated some immediate and radical upheaval in my life, but I knew I was headed for a change. Shortly thereafter, I turned down a very good business opportunity and increased my efforts to find something in the not-for-profit area. That took a long time. I also increased my volunteering, which led to full-time work with the church. I know that all those experiences prepared me for my work with Habitat for Humanity.

> HOLY DISCONTENT ... IS WHEN ... GOD SEIZES US SO THAT WE PUT DOWN THE REMOTE CONTROL AND FEEL AN URGENCY TO RESPOND.

A Call to Action

Many people have felt a similar call either to respond to the specific issue of poverty housing or to do something else tangible to put their faith into action. The latter is one of the reasons why Habitat for Humanity has had such an appeal for many people. Many local Habitat groups were first started in churches by people who say they believe God called them to the work of this ministry.

John Goodman, a military chaplain who traveled the world for many years ministering to troops, says that his retirement years working with Habitat have given him some of the most satisfying ministry experiences he has ever had.

"I retired from the military in 2000 after twenty-two years of active duty with the United States Air Force as a chaplain. What a great experience to wear the blue uniform, to travel all over the world, and to provide Christian ministry to our men and women in service. As I closed that chapter of my life in 2000 and returned to my home state of Arkansas, I truly wondered what God had in store for me that could be more fulfilling. Would he place me back in a pastorate? What would he want me to do?

"Today, as I look back, I am convinced beyond any doubt that he opened the door to this wonderful ministry we call Habitat for Humanity," Goodman said. "God closed other doors and opened this one, and I am so grateful that I walked through the threshold. Five years have passed, and I marvel. This is life-changing ministry!"

John Remington, construction supervisor in Holmes County, Ohio, served as a missionary in Eastern Europe during the Cold War distributing Bibles in very dangerous situations. Just as God called him to that service, Remington says he feels a passionate call today to serve God by building houses with God's children in need.

For three decades, hundreds of thousands of donors and volunteers all over the world have put their holy discontent to work with Habitat for Humanity. At some point they determined that it is unacceptable for poor families to struggle amid the hardships that poverty imposes and that it just won't do for children and their parents to live under leaky roofs or amid rodent infestation or with no water or sanitary facilities. Now Habitat for Humanity is at work in more than ninety countries around the world.

Matthew Maury, our vice-president serving in Africa and the Middle East, has said, "I personally have come to a deeper understanding of the fullness of the Good News— understanding in new ways the wholeness of Christ's message of the kingdom and his call for daily transformation in my own life as I serve alongside those he loves."

This call upon the lives of thousands of people has allowed us to be about so much more than building houses. Habitat for Humanity is a partner in building the kingdom that God intended for us.

I believe that of those to whom much has been given, much is expected. As we have been blessed, we are to be a blessing to others. Part of our own spiritual formation is the call to put our faith into action. Throughout Scripture, God mandates that faithful followers care for the poor.

- Deuteronomy 15:7-11 teaches that one should not be hardhearted or tightfisted toward those who are poor.
- Psalm 82:2-4 is clear that we are to care for the poor and needy.
- Proverbs 19:17 and Matthew 25:40 tell us that when

we minister to the poor, it is the same as serving the Lord.
- In Luke 19:8, Zacchaeus volunteered that as an act of repentance, he would give half his possessions to the poor.

For Christians, if we take Jesus seriously, we have to respond tangibly to the plight of the poor. How we respond—what we choose to do—is optional, but the call to conscience and obedience is not an option.

The Jewish faith teaches followers to repair the world, and followers of other faiths are urged to care for the poor as well. For some people compassionate response is not a matter of faith. It is simply the right thing to do, or it is part of the overall mind-set of an individual.

What about you? Are you ready to step out for the first time or to step out even further to show mercy to another?

Questions for Reflection

1. How would you describe mercy? What does it mean to love mercy as called for in Micah 6:8?

2. When have you been shown great mercy from other people? When has someone gone out of his or her way—truly dropped everything to help you?

3. When have you extended mercy (in the sense of showing compassion and taking action) to another person?

4. At the beginning of this chapter, you read about Mr. Chiochan and how the community went beyond simply

replacing the home he lost in the storm. They felt compelled to do something greater for him. Why do you think that is? When have you felt a need to personally respond to a great need? Why do you think you were drawn to the situation?

5. How would you explain the difference between concern and holy discontent?

6. What social issue troubles you? What can't you stand about the conditions or circumstances of a particular group of people? What are you going to do about it?

7. When have you felt God tug at your heart? What did you do?

8. Consider this statement: "If we take Jesus seriously, we have to respond tangibly to the plight of the poor." Do you agree or disagree? Why? What actions have you taken in obedience to Jesus' call to care for the poor?

Chapter 2
Called to Community

In some of my earliest travels with Habitat for Humanity, I visited the community of Al Motamadia, on the west side of Cairo. I had heard about the project, but nothing could have prepared me for what I encountered there. Immediately upon stepping out of the car, we were confronted with the pungent smell of everyday waste. It was like being placed in the middle of a Dumpster full of the discarded pieces of daily life. Piles of garbage lined the streets and were stacked in the entryways to the houses.

The families of Al Motamadia—including the children—go out on donkey carts each morning to collect the garbage from around the city and bring it back to their homes, where they sort through it for recyclables, which are in turn sold for cash. Children play near piles of trash; and pigs, chickens, and goats root in the piles for the tastiest morsels.

It was hard to imagine anyone living here, but this is their home, and their livelihood. Without this work, they would not be able to survive. The area includes schools, stores, and places of worship—it is their community.

The Coptic Evangelical Organization for Social Services introduced Habitat to the community. CEOSS is the largest Egyptian social service agency, involved in villages all over Egypt. (See page 34.) People in the Al Motamadia community expressed their desire for housing, but they also communicated three essential needs: They wanted a safe, humane place to live; they needed a place to rear their pigs; and they needed a place to do their work and sort garbage.

This was an important part of creating a successful partnership. Habitat for Humanity could help the people in the Al Motamadia community solve their problems, but the solution had to be respectful of the needs of the community. A local committee was formed and plans were drawn up according to people's desires and Habitat's healthy housing principles. Most of the new homes were two stories tall, with people living on the second floor and pigs and garbage sectioned off on the first. By coordinating local insight, national oversight, and international support, Habitat for Humanity Egypt was able to bring simple, decent, healthy housing to Al Motamadia.

People had been spending as much as 25 percent of their income just to purchase medicine. After acquiring housing, they could be proactive in fighting disease and could begin spending their money on education, clothing, and food.

> BY COORDINATING LOCAL INSIGHT, NATIONAL OVERSIGHT, AND INTERNATIONAL SUPPORT, HABITAT FOR HUMANITY EGYPT WAS ABLE TO BRING SIMPLE, DECENT, HEALTHY HOUSING TO AL MOTAMADIA.

One young man explained that he couldn't get married until he could provide a home for his new wife. The partnership with Habitat for

Humanity offered him that opportunity. He was willing to put in the sweat equity hours that are required of all Habitat home owners. He also agreed to repay a no-profit loan in the form of mortgage payments, also a fundamental principle of Habitat. He simply needed a chance to get started, a chance to provide a home for his family.

I visited the new home of Om Romani in the community. Previously, she lived with her husband and three children in a one-room shelter, just feet away from the piles of garbage they collected. As I walked up the stairs, the whiff of the piles still floated past my nose. But as soon as I stepped inside her house, the environment changed. The house was clean, beautifully painted and fresh—and there was no hint in the air that the house sat inside this busy garbage collector community.

The house made an incredible difference in her life, in her outlook, and in the health and future of her children. It fills my heart to see families who were living, literally, in garbage now live in an oasis above. And this transformation is taking place throughout the area, promoting dignity and respect and raising people up and out of poverty and despair. It is truly remarkable—thanks to this incredible partnership with CEOSS and the local community council that oversees and guides it.

Building Community

The program helped to raise the standard of living in Al Motamadia, with healthy houses ensuring healthier families. It also helped with unemployment, providing construction jobs for those who were not making a living in the collection of garbage. But the CEOSS partners here also told me of another, less tangible benefit.

"The community needs this program for the cohesiveness it brings," one person said. "It has changed the village so much that even these families, whom some might consider living on the brink of poverty, are pulling together to buy houses for people who cannot afford a loan."

Many of the leaders in Egypt explained that often what draws people to Habitat is not necessarily the building of the house but the importance of the house in building a community. At one meeting, representatives provided background on the local organizations and Habitat affiliates and told how Habitat had changed the lives of families and transformed their communities. Each story was more heartwarming than the last, but all spoke of the positive effect the Habitat program has on the community as a whole—forging ties where none existed, building capacity for more development, and empowering the people to continue working toward a better future. With a loan repayment rate of 97 percent, Habitat home owners are active participants in extending housing opportunities to more potential family partners.

> MANY OF THE LEADERS IN EGYPT EXPLAINED THAT OFTEN WHAT DRAWS PEOPLE TO HABITAT IS NOT NECESSARILY THE BUILDING OF THE HOUSE BUT THE IMPORTANCE OF THE HOUSE IN BUILDING A COMMUNITY.

Some of the most remarkable stories were those that brought Christians and Muslims together. In one case, a Christian family's home was demolished to make room for the new Habitat home under construction. The family was to be homeless for three months, but the local Imam, also a

Habitat home owner, took the family in. The Imam admitted that initially it was difficult for him, but the love he was shown by Habitat was so special he wanted to show that same love to others. What an amazing testimony of hands reaching across faiths to build communities! What an expression of mercy!

Another great example of real community transformation can be found in the United States in Jackson, Mississippi. In 1993, Habitat for Humanity/Metro Jackson made the decision to concentrate its efforts in one neighborhood to increase the impact of the homes being built. Rows of vacant shotgun shacks were replaced by new houses with neatly trimmed lawns. Where drug dealers once filled the streets, children walk home safely from school. Thirteen years later Habitat had built more than 180 homes in the Midtown neighborhood.

The success of this effort led to the creation of a new vision for inner-city neighborhoods, and in 2003 the affiliate announced the Nehemiah Project, which was an initiative to build 100 homes in a three-year period. The goal of this project was to revitalize neighborhoods and reduce crime, while affecting businesses, schools, and the entire city. Habitat's commitment to inner-city neighborhoods was an effort to strengthen the downtown area by stabilizing blighted areas with home owners.

An Attitude of Mercy

Imagine such initiatives in every community. Building houses is just one way to inaugurate change. Imagine what the world would look like if more and more people were to become passionate about improving the lives of others. Imagine if countless people began to practice outrageous generosity. What if entire regions adopted a manner of mercy? How would housing and other social issues change where you live? How would housing challenges change around the world?

> KEPT UNTO OURSELVES, OUR GIFTS DO NOT HAVE THE SAME IMPACT AS THEY DO WHEN THEY ARE OF-FERED TO GOD TO BE USED IN ACTS OF COMPASSION AND CARING.

Many countries of the world have been very generous in offering aid for extreme poverty and global AIDS victims, but an attitude of mercy calls for even more to provide basic needs like health, education, clean water, and food to transform and further the hopes of an entire generation in the world's poorest countries.

First Corinthians 12 encourages this kind of universal caring for one another. The Apostle Paul says we are all part of the body of Christ, called to use each of our gifts to serve together. We were never intended to use our gifts apart from God's purposes. In fact, verse 18 says that God arranged all the parts of the body in a very specific way. God designed us to cooperate together. Kept to ourselves, our gifts do not have the same impact as they do when they are offered to God to be used in acts of compassion and caring.

Creative Innovations

Habitat for Humanity is entering its fourth decade, and one of our challenges as we go forward is to stay true to our core principles while also finding new ways to affect the growing problem of poverty housing. We partner with families, emphasizing respect and dignity. That is fundamental. The fact that we ask families to put in sweat equity and pay a mortgage is also fundamental.

If we look at a family that is earning $1 a day, however—and sadly, there are a billion such families out there in the world—they probably cannot afford a fifteen-year mortgage on even a very inexpensive home. So we have to adapt our model and look at ideas such as microfinancing. Habitat for Humanity is just one organization that helps extremely poor families have access to very small loans for house building or for developing their businesses or for other activities to improve their lives. The very poor lack access to traditional financing, so these small loans from nontraditional sources are essential.

One of the things we are doing is developing a model called Building in Stages, whereby we make a series of home improvement loans that enable a family to improve their home one step at a time.

We might make a very small loan and work with a family to get a galvanized aluminum roof on their home, which would be a major step forward for the quality of their lives. The next year we might work with them and put a concrete floor in, which does wonders for the health and cleanliness of the home. The next step might be to add another room so that they can have the boys and the girls in different rooms.

We are partnering with microfinance organizations for home improvement loans, leveraging the fact that they have loan management and expertise already in place. One model is for them to provide the home improvement loan and for us to work with the family on physically improving the home. Another model is for the microfinance organization to work with the family to give them credit so that they can create a business that would help them pay for a home that they build with Habitat for Humanity.

Our principle is that it is good for families to participate in building their home, paying for their home, and owning their home. But it is critical that we keep the cost low enough so that they can afford it with a reasonable percentage of their income.

Transformation and Sustainable Community Development

Our Save & Build program is another way that we partner with communities to serve the very poor. Pioneered by HFH Sri Lanka, Save & Build brings together low-income families in a community to form savings groups.

It was Save & Build that allowed Sarath Tikiribandara to complete a simple, decent house for his family. Sarath, his wife, and their three children had lived in a mud hut for more than ten years. He dreamed of a secure home where they could sleep safely and where the children's schoolbooks would stay dry. He had managed to invest in a foundation for the home and had started making bricks on his own. But as he was working on the bricks one day, Sarath was bitten by a poisonous snake. Weeks in intensive care and months in the hospital put an end to the building for more than four years.

Sarath met a member of a Habitat for Humanity savings group and heard about Save & Build. He went to a meeting and learned more about the program. "I didn't know the other members of the group before, but we all wanted a house," Sarath said. "Now we have close ties and fruitful relationships."

Members of the Save & Build group saved fifteen to twenty rupees a day. They also collected building materials and made their own bricks. When the group had enough building materials compiled and enough money raised, Habitat for Humanity matched their funds, and house building began. As with all Habitat houses, the families contributed labor, or sweat equity, and hired masons to do some of the more specialized work. The cycle of saving, collecting, building, and loan repayment continued until all members of the group had a house. Members of the group had the option to begin the cycle again and add rooms to their houses.

During construction, local affiliate coordinator Prageeth Jayantha Perera pointed out a coconut hanging from a bush near the building site. "The group hung it there when they started building," he said. "When the house was to be dedicated, they planned to break it, scrape out the meat, and boil it over the fire until it overflowed. That was to celebrate the abundance and prosperity for this family in a new home."

Sarath recognized the symbolism in his fresh start and new house, but he was more concerned with the concrete reality. He held his youngest daughter tightly and admired the blocks and bricks he made that will protect her as she grows up.

This building of communities is the essence of what we do at Habitat for Humanity. Constructing houses is simply the means by which we do it. In Indonesia, I witnessed a fascinating community process take place after the entire village was washed away by the tsunami. Before anyone could begin to rebuild houses, the people had to determine where property lines were located. Without any points of reference, that was very difficult. The villagers, however, worked together and began to agree on where they believed their property began and ended.

This new level of cooperation was required before solutions could begin. If the community had chosen to rely upon the government to reconstruct property lines when all the records had been destroyed, the process would likely have taken months if not years to complete. However, because neighbors worked together, the property lines were established in a matter of weeks.

IN INDONESIA, I WITNESSED A FASCINATING COMMUNITY PROCESS TAKE PLACE AFTER THE ENTIRE VILLAGE WAS WASHED AWAY BY THE TSUNAMI.... THIS NEW LEVEL OF COOPERATION WAS REQUIRED BEFORE SOLUTIONS COULD BEGIN.

Families planted stakes to mark the boundaries of what they believed to be their land and then put up hand-painted signs with their family names on them. All neighbors had to sign a letter as verification that these boundaries were authentic. When that process was complete, the letters were authorized by the leader of that section of the village. Those letters with rudimentary drawings and boundary indications were converted to hand-drawn section maps. The section maps were compiled into a single community map to be approved by public works and subdistrict leaders. Community groups handled any disagreements. Local Habitat leaders facilitated the process, but the community owned the solution.

This coming together, this personal involvement of neighbor helping neighbor to respond to a pressing need, was amazing. Certainly, in this case, everyone benefited, but the overwhelming tragedy led people to think beyond themselves and to think about rebuilding the community.

Reconciliation

Another element of building community and finding solutions that has been part of Habitat for Humanity's story
from the beginning has been the idea of reconciliation. From
our roots at Koinonia Farm, where Christians sought to live
in racial harmony, to some of our current projects that bring
together Muslims, Christians, and Jews who seek an ave-
nue for building peace, Habitat for Humanity has been an
opportunity to put aside differences and to work together.
Habitat projects have brought together unlikely partners on
construction sites around the world. Transformation occurs
not only in the lives of those who live in the houses but also
in the lives of those who build.

Each year former U.S. President Jimmy Carter hosts a
building project that attracts volunteers from around the
world. In 2006, the Jimmy Carter Work Project was in India.
President Carter and I were working in the city of Lonavala
just outside of Mumbai alongside volunteers from many
countries and faiths, building a duplex for two low-income
families, one Hindu and one Muslim. At the dedication,
Aziz, one home owner, said of his new neighbor, Subhash,
"We are of different castes and different faiths, but now we
are brothers."

Pakistani and Indian students working on a house together
also began to notice what they had in common rather than
focusing on their differences. "We look alike, and even though
we speak different languages, we can understand one another,"
one said as they built more than walls together.

Reconciliation is a major emphasis for Habitat's work in
Northern Ireland, too, where for centuries sectarianism choked
the channels of peace, tolerance, and understanding. In the

process of declaring their respective identities, many Catholics and Protestants long cultivated a hatred of one another—a hatred that countless times manifested itself in violence, shootings, bombings, kidnappings, torture, riots, and murder.

In a land like Northern Ireland, Habitat quickly takes on a special meaning; it assumes an extraordinary context. For Habitat partners there, a decent, affordable home is not so much an end in itself as a means to an end—a vehicle through which Catholics and Protestants, historically so intensely divided, can come together in peace.

Every Habitat house built in Northern Ireland is done so through the combined sweat and hands of both Catholics and Protestants. So while the region right now remains too deeply scarred for an integrated neighborhood, the efforts, goals, and successes of Habitat-Northern Ireland are fully woven in a cloth of mutual respect and inclusion. Through Habitat, each side fosters a connection with the other.

Once again, mercy calls for individuals to look beyond human restraints and to respond to God's call to show extraordinary compassion and to love as we have been loved.

Take the First Step

Habitat for Humanity supporters are working to help people find solutions to their problems in communities around the world. What about you? My goal is to ignite in people a greater sense of purpose—to help people personally experience how others live—to see the face of extreme poverty. Get out into the community and put yourself in a position where you can see what is wrong. Create space for the Spirit to move. Not everyone can travel great distances, but you can take the first step. Work in a food kitchen or help with a Habitat house. Cross socioeconomic lines. It is transformational to build alongside hardworking folks who want the same things in life that you do.

You may be going to India or you may be going across the railroad tracks, but it means getting up and doing something. There is an obedience piece to this, too. It is hard to read the gospel

> GET OUT INTO THE COM-
> MUNITY AND PUT YOURSELF
> IN A POSITION WHERE YOU
> CAN SEE WHAT IS WRONG.
> CREATE SPACE FOR THE
> SPIRIT TO MOVE.

and not believe we are called to reach out to our neighbor, and that is a broad definition of neighbor.

Questions for Reflection

1. Do you consider yourself active in your community or small communities, or are you rather insulated? How about your church or group?

2. Do you have examples of working closely with individuals or groups to respect their needs while trying to help them find solutions to problems (like the community in Egypt that needed a space to sort the garbage)?

3. How sensitive do you consider yourself when interacting with people who are very different from you? How about your church/group?

4. What examples can you give of people who have worked in your community to bring about reconciliation?

5. Does the idea of a decent house for everyone create a feeling of urgency within you? If so, what ideas are stirring in your heart and mind?

6. What experiences have you or others had in observing people come together in community to solve their problems? What are some common factors in those experiences?

7. In what specific communities can you envision people working together to transform themselves? What must they do? What resources do they need?

Habitat for Humanity and the Coptic Evangelical Organization for Social Services

The partnership between Habitat for Humanity Egypt and the Coptic Evangelical Organization for Social Services is a very fruitful and wonderful model. CEOSS is a national leader in helping Egyptians articulate their needs, acquire the resources to meet those needs, and develop the capacity locally to implement solutions.

CEOSS works through community-based organizations (CBOs) in poor areas. Depending on the demographics of the community, the board of directors and staff of the community organizations may be Muslim or Christian or both. The CBOs know that CEOSS is a Christian organization because it has worked for more than fifty years in many communities in Egypt, and its reputation is well known. Thus, the CBOs know that CEOSS is doing its work because Jesus asked Christians to care for the poor and to work for justice in this life. However, they also know that CEOSS will respect religious diversity. This selfless love is a powerful testimony to the CBOs and the community residents.

To begin the work, CEOSS, in conjunction with the local CBO, organizes the work of the community residents by dividing them into groups regardless of religion, gender, or color. CEOSS teaches the groups about the mission and goals of both Habitat and CEOSS to encourage them to help themselves and to care for their neighbors by working in teams, not as individuals. A decision-making committee is formed to choose the beneficiaries of the homes and to identify available resources in the area. This committee also develops a plan of cooperation among residents to prepare, build, and finish the houses.

Another role of this committee is to encourage wealthier residents of the village to help either by providing raw materials at reasonable prices or by facilitating the building permits. Throughout the residents' participation in the process, the moral dimension is stressed to give accurate information, to identify objective criteria for choosing the first beneficiaries, and to avoid any kind of discrimination.

Throughout the work process and the daily interaction, strong relationships are established between citizens of the same community and between residents and the governmental officials and executives—even if they are of different backgrounds.

As this process repeats and because of daily coexistence, a spirit of cooperation is built and trust and hope increase, especially for the segments of the community that are most in need.

Habitat home owner Veronica Addai at her Habitat house in Ghana.

PART TWO
HOUSING
AND JUSTICE

Injustice anywhere is a threat to justice everywhere. We are caught in an inescapable network of mutuality, tied in a single garment of destiny. What affects one directly, affects all indirectly.

—*Martin Luther King Jr., Letter from the Birmingham Jail, April 16, 1963*

This flood–damaged house sat empty for eight months following Hurricane Katrina. Volunteers, in coordination with New Orleans Area Habitat for Humanity and other organizations, will "muck" the house, clearing it of debris.

Chapter 3
Called to Bring Hope

"No one ever plans to end up on the streets, but that is what happened to me. I only planned to be in a homeless shelter temporarily, but I ended up staying there three years. I couldn't find my niche in life, and the streets were addicting. Then I got pregnant. I knew I couldn't care for a child, and I didn't want to change my life, so my mother in Texas raised my son."

When Cynthia Winn became pregnant a second time, however, she said her mother told her she needed to grow up and be a mom. "I was very poor, but I knew I had to get off the streets, so I moved into some raggedy apartments because of my child," said Winn. "When you decide to make a big change, you can't be afraid. You have to take the first step."

A friend at work told Winn about Habitat for Humanity, but she admits that she was turned off by the idea of hammering and working to build her own house. "I just didn't want to do that. Plus, I knew my credit was not good and I didn't think I would ever have anything."

However, she decided to apply for a home and was amazed at the reception she received from the staff and supporters at the Habitat for Humanity affiliate in Columbia, South Carolina. "They gave me a second chance," she said, "and that is something I wanted so badly."

When Habitat representatives came for a home visit, Winn said they made her feel special. "My heart just grew. Beforehand, I didn't trust anyone, but when I realized that this was for real and I was really going to have a house, I was overwhelmed. This was more than I could ever imagine."

Habitat supporters transported Winn to meetings and helped her get through the process of being approved for a home. "I knew this was more than just a program. The people really cared about me. I began some counseling and started blossoming. I also started going to church and soon was baptized. It was so wonderful. The Lord had a hand in all this and accepted me with open arms."

Winn's journey has not been without struggle, however. Her abusive boyfriend did not like her new confidence and strength. "It was difficult, but I had to get away from him. You cannot continue to do the things that you know are not good for you and expect God to bless you."

Winn also faced health problems and has sought help for her youngest son, Kareem, who is autistic. Kareem, who is now in school, is doing well, and Winn is on the dean's list at Benedict College in Columbia. Working and going to school are difficult, but Winn is determined to earn her degree in elementary education. She said she is so grateful to all those who have helped her. "I get on my knees and thank God. I know God has blessed me so much. Go for your blessing," she urges. "God will deliver you."

A Message of Hope

When people perceive that they have no possibility to better their situations, they are willing to do desperate things. Sometimes they simply give up. However, when people believe that they can experience positive changes in their lives, they have reasons to look forward. Prisoners of war, in the worst of conditions, have found strength to make it through endless days of separation and bleakness—even torture—because they had hope that one day they would see freedom. Cynthia Winn discovered that she could build a better life for herself and for her son, so she continues to set goals and to work hard to achieve them. She has experienced success. She knows firsthand the meaning of hope.

Poverty can be a constant battle against hopelessness, but Job 5:16 says, "The poor have hope, and injustice shuts its mouth." The psalmist proclaims, "I will always have hope" (Psalm 71:14).

> PRISONERS OF WAR, IN THE WORST OF CONDITIONS, HAVE FOUND STRENGTH TO MAKE IT THROUGH ENDLESS DAYS OF SEPARATION AND BLEAKNESS—EVEN TORTURE—BECAUSE THEY HAD HOPE THAT ONE DAY THEY WOULD SEE FREEDOM.

Habitat for Humanity is about building hope—about removing barriers and creating opportunities. By being the hands and feet of Jesus in the world, we can bring hope to those who are seeking a way to improve their circumstances. The cleanup efforts following Hurricane Katrina are a perfect example.

Col. Dave Dysart, U.S. Marine reservist heading the St. Bernard Parish Recovery Project in New Orleans following the storm, told what a difference hope made in that community.

When some of the first teams started working, their job was to gut out the water-soaked houses to help families who were going to return to their homes to rebuild.

Dysart said his team had cleaned out hundreds of houses in St. Bernard Parish, and Habitat for Humanity volunteers had a great presence in getting the work started. "You cannot measure the progress of our work by only the houses that we have done, but you have to look at the houses near our work, where people have decided that since houses nearby have been gutted, they can come back and start working on their houses," he said.

In many cases, however, "For Sale" signs were popping up in the yards. "It was not our desire to gut the homes of individuals so that they could sell them. That was not our mission. We were trying to help residents return to their homes as quickly as possible."

He pointed out that when Habitat for Humanity builds a typical house with a home owner, there is tremendous benefit of working together on the house during construction. With families displaced by the hurricane, however, the situation was a little different.

"Down here, the people the volunteers were helping were living in Texas. Volunteers were taking gunk, debris, and mud out of the house. It was not so rewarding for them, nor did they get the interaction with the home owner. So we made it a point to call our residents and tell them we would appreciate it if they would come down and participate in the process and collect any remaining personal items."

One gentleman, who was about sixty years old, returned alone to help clean out his home. He said he could not get his wife to come back to the area because it was too hard for her to see everything that they owned completely destroyed.

"Everything we had was tied up in this house," the man said, adding that the cleanup process was difficult for him as well. He said he appreciated what everyone was doing and that if the team could help him find a few trinkets, he and his wife could start their lives over somewhere else.

However, an amazing change of heart took place after the house was gutted and everything was cleaned out of his house. The man went to the front yard and pulled the "For Sale" sign out of the ground and threw it on top of the debris. "You all taught me that there are people who love me. You've taught me that there are people around this world that want to see me come home, and me and my wife can come home now," he said. He began the process of rebuilding his house.

The incredible thing about hope is that it is relative. Research has shown that often a person's outlook on life is less about one's actual circumstance but rather about whether an individual believes he or she is progressing or has the potential to improve.

When a person experiences the care and compassion of others, often he or she has a new understanding of the world. When total strangers dig a well or serve in a soup kitchen or build houses, their acts of compassion can change lives. A sense of community develops when people get involved.

Sometimes those awkward first moments give way to lifelong friendships. Atlanta home owner Evelyn Jackson asked Lynn Merrill why she would come out and dig footings for her house in the red Georgia clay. "You don't even know me," she proclaimed.

Merrill replied that working on the house was an op-

> WHEN A PERSON EXPE-
> RIENCES THE CARE AND
> COMPASSION OF OTHERS,
> OFTEN HE OR SHE HAS A
> NEW UNDERSTANDING OF
> THE WORLD.

portunity to live out her faith. The two women became close friends over the years. "We have married our children and buried our parents together," Merrill said. "Evelyn has taught me courage, kindness, thoughtfulness, and willingness."

The ability to offer hope is at the heart of Habitat for Humanity. Our philosophy is not to play God with people's lives but rather to partner with families to give them a chance to move out of poverty, to gain assets, and to give their children a chance to have a healthy environment in which to grow. I am convinced that every person ought to have the opportunity to have a safe, decent place in which to live. Helping to create that opportunity, I believe, is a way in which we can seek to create a just world as advocated by the prophet Micah.

When people feel surrounded by those who want to help them solve their own problems, lasting transformation takes place. This creates dignity and lasting independence.

The Issue of Poverty Housing

"One in three American households spends more than 30 percent of income on housing and one in seven spends more than 50 percent. The growing shortage of affordable units forces millions of families to make difficult choices to pay for housing—sacrifice other basic needs, make long commutes, and/or live in crowded or inadequate conditions."[1] Working families are struggling in many areas to find an affordable place to live. A full-time worker at minimum wage cannot afford a modest one-bedroom apartment anywhere in the country, and 90 percent of renter households in the United States live in counties where the median wage—$12.22 nationally—is not sufficient to cover the cost of a modest two-bedroom rental unit.[2]

Fifty years ago, most families could buy a home at roughly double their income. Now that ratio can be eight or nine to one in some places. We talk about the affordability index, which is the ability for a median income family to afford a medium cost home in a community. That index is at the worst level it has been since the nation has been keeping statistics.

> ONE IN THREE AMERI-
> CAN HOUSEHOLDS SPENDS
> MORE THAN 30 PERCENT
> OF INCOME ON HOUSING
> AND ONE IN SEVEN SPENDS
> MORE THAN 50 PERCENT.

Nic Retsinas, director of Harvard University's Joint Center for Housing Studies, says that families in America are experiencing a broken social contract. "For many years, the understanding was that once I get a job, everything will be fine, but now having a job does not guarantee having a decent place to live," he said. Throughout the United States, the rising cost of housing is outpacing the increase in wages for many laborers.

Owning a home is out of reach for many people. Habitat for Humanity is the leading national housing provider that targets families who are at an income level of 40 to 60 percent below the median.

The Importance of Housing

Historically, when people think poverty, they think food, water, health care, and education. All these are essential. However, what is often left out is housing, and what we are finding out is that housing is critical to all the factors that affect the poor. Millard Fuller, founder of Habitat for Humanity International, said, "I have always felt that a house is to a human family what soil is to a plant. You can pull a plant up out of the soil, pour all the water in the world on it, give it plenty of sunlight, and it will eventually die because it is not rooted. A plant needs to be rooted. A family is like that. If a family is not rooted, it will not flourish. It will not grow . . . will not blossom. But once a family is well-rooted, all kinds of wonderful things will begin to happen."

We find that adequate housing significantly affects health, for example. A study of the effects of Habitat for Humanity housing in northern Malawi concluded that the incidence of respiratory, gastrointestinal, or malarial illnesses was reduced by 44 percent in those children living in Habitat for Humanity houses compared to those living in nearby traditional houses.[3]

In another study where Habitat for Humanity families in Costa Rica were interviewed, 88 percent reported improvements in general health. Some noted that the cement walls and floors sealed the house better and kept out the dampness; others explained improved health due to cleanliness, lack of rodents, and fewer people living in the house. Thirty-eight percent of the families reported that their children were doing better in school, and 39 percent reported that their children had developed a more positive attitude toward school.[4]

I saw firsthand the difference that a healthy home can make when I visited a young family in Romania shortly after they had moved. Nicolae Angelescu, his wife Ioana-Mariana and their two-year-old daughter Alexandra-Gabriela had previously lived in a small 2 x 3 square-meter apartment that was cold, damp, and entirely inadequate. "It was terrible," Nicolae told me quite simply. Young Alexandra-Gabriela had contracted pneumonia twice in their previous home.

Today they live modestly in a clean apartment, paying one-quarter of what they used to pay in rent and occupying a space five times as large. "We just wanted to have our own roof on top of our heads," Nicolae told me. "We just wanted our own shelter."

And in Durban, South Africa, I talked with a home owner whose life was completely changed by having a safe and decent place to live. "There is not crime here," Roanne Dennis told me. "I can leave washing outside to dry. If it starts to rain, a neighbor will take it inside for me if I'm gone. In other places, the laundry would just disappear." Most important, her children are safe and healthy. Before moving into this house, she rented a rat-infested room in town with her two children, ages thirteen and eleven, and her mother. Her son, who has a learning disability, became ill from a rat bite. Today he is healthy and surrounded by neighbors who also watch out for his safety.

"We worked hard for this house," she said. "We got to know our neighbors as we all worked together on the weekends on our houses. That's why we are so close. We all know each other and their children. We know where they belong."

In the United States, findings indicate that children of home owners are more likely to graduate from high school and college and have higher math and reading scores, fewer behavioral problems, and fewer alcohol and substance abuse problems than do the children of renters. They are also less likely to become pregnant as teenagers.[5]

Bringing Housing to the Forefront

The incredible international disasters of 2004–2005 brought poverty to a worldwide stage as people from many nations were mesmerized by the destruction wrought by the tsunami in Asia and the hurricanes in the Gulf region of the United

States. People responded overwhelmingly to relief efforts, and their eyes were opened to the fact that many of the world's citizens struggled in unacceptable living conditions long before the storms struck.

People intuitively understand that housing is critical, but it is less visceral than issues such as illness or not having clean water to drink. Other housing-related issues are more difficult to address, but they are nonetheless critical quality-of-life matters, such as young girls living in the same room with older men.

Responding to housing need is hard, and it is expensive and daunting. We at Habitat for Humanity have been in the business of building affordable housing around the world for more than thirty years. On the one hand, we celebrate that we have partnered with countless people to build more than 200,000 homes; yet there are still over a billion people living in poverty conditions. Two hundred thousand is an amazing figure, but it is miniscule compared to the problem. We are going to have to expand our thinking to include new possibilities and partnerships that fit with our core principles of partnering with individual families.

We have committed ourselves to become advocates and catalysts with other partners so that we can build exponentially more houses. We will also raise public awareness for affordable housing and advocate for policies and practices that produce and preserve affordable housing around the world.

We balance our large-scale strategy with the reminder that we partner with individual families and communities. Always crucial to the ministry of Habitat will be people like Cynthia Winn, who found her way off the streets, and Nicolae Angelescu, whose family sought a healthy home in which to live.

Habitat for Humanity helps people find hope through affordable housing; others work to alleviate hunger or to find cures for diseases or to support education or many other endeavors. How can you help bring hope to someone who is feeling discouraged?

Reflection Questions

1. When have you experienced feelings of hopelessness? What are some images or descriptions that describe hopelessness?

2. Cynthia Winn said she never planned to end up on the streets. Have you ever found yourself following a path that you never expected? If so, describe your journey. If this was an undesirable detour, how did you get back on track?

3. When have you experienced an amazing opportunity that caused you to suddenly feel hopeful when you did not expect it? What was your reaction?

4. Are you more likely to respond to a tragedy than to an ongoing situation, such as poverty housing? Explain.

5. What experiences do you know about when adequate housing made a radical difference in someone's life?

6. Whom do you know that might be feeling some degree of hopelessness? What might you do to help?

Habitat home owner Lois Witcher's new home sits behind her old home.

Chapter 4
Called to Understand

Childhood innocence quickly disappeared for Alverna Walker. When Walker's mother passed away, Walker, only seven years old at the time, became "Mom" to her siblings. At age thirteen, she and her family moved in with a cousin in search of a stable home environment.

Although moving provided a safe place to live, Walker then shared a small house with sixteen other family members. Walker almost added to that number when she became pregnant at age sixteen, but she decided it was time to make a life of her own and moved into her late great-grandfather's house.

"It was like a shack, with no real running water and bathrooms, indoor toilets," Walker says. "I started working and pursuing and looking hard for the things that I needed."

Walker applied for a Habitat house.

As her girls grew up on Habitat Boulevard, Walker again seized the opportunity to make a better life for her daughters Katina, Bridget, and Annette. She encouraged them to take advantage of a quiet home by studying hard and succeeding in school.

"Your environment is who you are," Walker says. "The environment that you live in plays a big part [in shaping] your children and yourself. My children did great in school . . . and I really feel it was because of the environment. If they had to struggle with no running water and all that, that would affect them somewhere down the line."

Walker paid off her mortgage early and refinanced her home. The appreciation on her house paid for each of her daughters to continue studying after high school. She shines with pride when she speaks of her children's accomplishments, their marriages, and her grandchildren. But there is another source of pride for Walker.

"I always wanted to go to college," she says. "I work for the county. I have a good job. Those are some of the things I can look back and say God has truly blessed me in."

Walker is an ordained pastor and is now pursuing a master's degree in early childhood education while working with drug-addicted babies. And because of her experiences, she now wants to open a shelter for women.

Looking back on her first sixteen years of life, Walker says with hope, "Yes, I had a hard life, but all that worked together for my good; it really did."

The Root Causes of Poverty and Substandard Housing

Many individuals and groups have done exhaustive studies on the causes of poverty and the factors that contribute to its perpetuation. Definitions of "poor" and "poverty level" and "causes of poverty," as opposed to "factors that contribute to poverty," become increasingly complex. It depends on whose lens you look through to determine why some people and some groups cannot break the cycle.

Sometimes poverty is the result of making poor choices. Unexpected events, such as the death of Alverna Walker's mother when Alverna was a child, can also thrust individuals and families into circumstances that seem hopeless unless there is some intervention.

1. Family History. In researching root causes of poverty, the Central Oregon Partnership listed as its number one factor a family history of poverty. They noted, "When one grows up surrounded by poverty, it's often the only environment they know, and when, in turn, they grow up, it's the environment they most often re-create in their own families." A cycle of dependency often develops. This is an internal restraint—what people believe about themselves.

Other restraints are more external—imposed by outside influences or factors.

2. Unequal access to assets. Assets include land, credit, information, education, resources, transportation, technology, and health care. Some countries are landlocked and have no access to rivers, for example. Other assets are less tangible.

Many of the poor in developing countries possess focus, talent, and enthusiasm, and they have an astonishing ability to wring a profit out of very little. However, Peruvian economist Hernando DeSoto says they lack the ability to establish liquid assets. If an economic system does not make opportunities for creating assets and capital, people cannot participate in economic growth.

This is precisely what Clarence Jordan, who is often called the spiritual father of Habitat for Humanity, was proposing when he first suggested the idea of partnership housing: "What the poor need is not charity but capital, not caseworkers but co-workers."

The ability to establish clear property titles—to track ownership over an asset—is another key factor in economic growth, DeSoto says. "Markets and capitalism are about trading property rights. It's about building capital or loans on property rights. What we've forgotten, because we've never examined the poor, we've sort of thought that the poor were a cultural problem, is that the poor don't have property rights. They have things, but not the rights. And when you don't have the rights, you don't have a piece of paper with which to go to market."[1]

Others argue simply that secure tenure, the confidence that you will not be unlawfully evicted whether or not you hold the title to the land where you live, also has a positive impact on quality of life. The United Nations Centre for Human Settlements has developed a Global Campaign for Secure Tenure that has the specific goal of reducing poverty. The Centre maintains that individuals who have a long-term mind-set can invest their time and resources toward improving their living and economic conditions. Such investments are hardly worth the effort if one is constantly living under the threat of eviction. Supporters are seeking to help the poor use secure tenure itself as collateral for obtaining loans. By helping to raise the status of those living in informal settlements, the UN group seeks to help bring the poor into formal communities and to help them benefit economically from the value of their land.

The importance of knowing you can stay in your home is emphasized in a study by two Argentine universities and Harvard Business School. An article in the *Wall Street Journal* in 2005 cited two families in San Francisco Solano, a barrio settled by squatters almost twenty-five years ago on the fringes of Buenos Aires. Both families lived on lots of the same size and earned similar incomes. Their stories are largely the same.

Mercedes Almada and her family of six live in a neat, colonial-style home with a slab roof supported with strong pillars. All family members have their own rooms. One daughter has finished high school and a son finished technical school.

Valentín Orellana's family of eight live in a house of rough cinder blocks and concrete with a corrugated zinc roof. They are so cramped that some family members sleep in the dining room and kitchen. None of the children have progressed past the seventh grade in school.

What is the difference? The research project attributes much of the disparity to the fact that Mrs. Almada held the title to her home; Mr. Orellana did not.

> The Argentine study followed 1,800 squatter families who in 1981 occupied a one-square-mile piece of what they assumed was public land. It had once served as a garbage dump. Through a quirk of the legal system, roughly half of the settlers in the heart of the neighborhood gained title to their properties, while the other half didn't. The researchers found that over the course of two decades, the title holders surpassed those without them in a host of key social indicators, ranging from quality of house construction to educational performance to rates of teenage pregnancy.
>
> Households with titles didn't earn more money than those without them and had access to only a modest amount more credit. Nevertheless, they adopted a more

entrepreneurial mindset and shucked the fatalism and fear of being tossed off their land that mark the poor throughout the region. They believed hard work would pay off for their families.[2]

Certainly access to education is also a key issue concerning poverty. At an international workshop on education and poverty eradication held in 2001 in Kampala, Uganda, organizers said, "The role of education in poverty eradication, in close co-operation with other social sectors, is crucial. No country has succeeded if it has not educated its people. Not only is education important in reducing poverty, it is also a key to wealth creation."[3]

3. Social capital. A third broad category that explains the perpetuation of poverty is that the poor often have limited social capital. They have little power and influence on decision-making groups. Governments may not invest in the poorest of the poor. The poor may not receive medical assistance and nutritional aid. If every bit of energy is spent on survival, people have nothing left to give to communities and to investing in their futures. To make matters worse, the struggle to get by can make them victims of corruption and usurious moneylenders. Ironically, governments may also fail to recognize the wealth of their own poor.

Social capital also includes social status and basic rights. In some societies, religious and cultural norms may limit the roles of women and, therefore, deprive them of their rights to land. This, in turn, prevents

> THE POOR MAY NOT RECEIVE MEDICAL ASSISTANCE AND NUTRITIONAL AID. IF EVERY BIT OF ENERGY IS SPENT ON SURVIVAL, PEOPLE HAVE NOTHING LEFT TO GIVE TO COMMUNITIES AND TO INVESTING IN THEIR FUTURES.

them from accessing adequate housing. Widows and single mothers are particularly vulnerable. In many countries property can only be recorded in a man's name. Exclusion of women from land pushes them toward the cities, where they join increasing numbers of female-headed households in the slums.[4]

Throughout the developing world, governments are beginning to change property rights laws. In Namibia, for example, the Married Persons Equality Act of 1996 gave women the right to their husbands' property after their death.[5]

Violence against women is a global issue that traps women in poverty housing. The HIV/AIDS pandemic, which has left many widows and orphans in desperate circumstances, has also exacerbated the poverty issue in many areas.

A Habitat team in Mozambique was particularly struck by this reality. They planned to build ten Habitat houses near the town of Chimoio, home of many HIV/AIDS orphans. The houses were built on a plot of land designated for children (and grandparents or substitute mothers) who have been living in extremely poor and vulnerable conditions.

Curious about the current living conditions of the children, five of the volunteers set off with local guides on a walk into the village to visit the homes that would be replaced. Soon the group came upon a small tentlike structure, no more than a few feet tall, made of sticks, plastic bags and a reed mat. Inside lived an elderly widow. She greeted the villagers slowly with hands shaking from what some suggested was Parkinson's disease.

A pastor explained that seventy-year-old Saquina Antonio lived in the village for years until her husband died. Afterward, she moved to Chimoio City to live with her daughter and son-in-law. Soon though, they both became sick and died, leaving Saquina with her niece. When her niece married, the new husband did not want to take care of his wife's aunt, so she moved back to the village, the only place where people would care to help her. She is one of the forgotten victims of HIV.

Fortunately, the villagers, who mostly lived in mud and thatch homes and fought to feed their own children, helped her to set up the make-shift home and gave her food, knowing she no longer could farm her own garden. When asked how she was, she responded, "Fine. Just waiting for God to take me."

Upon returning to the work site, group members sat down with the pastor to estimate the cost of building Saquina a mud hut. They collected $200, enough to include a cement floor and some basic food items to keep Saquina healthy and warm. The teams personally delivered extra clothes and blankets.

4. Natural disasters and unexpected events. As we saw in the devastating tsunami, hurricanes, and earthquakes of recent years, entire communities can be displaced. Many people lost everything and had to start their lives over again. Floods, crop failures, plant closings, illnesses, and diseases are other unanticipated events that can change the lives of individuals and whole populations without warning.

> AS WE SAW IN THE DEVASTATING TSUNAMI, HURRICANES, AND EARTHQUAKES OF RECENT YEARS, ENTIRE COMMUNITIES CAN BE DISPLACED. . . . UNANTICIPATED EVENTS . . . CAN CHANGE THE LIVES OF INDIVIDUALS AND WHOLE POPULATIONS WITHOUT WARNING.

5. Subjugation and oppression. A final explanation of why people become trapped in poverty is perhaps the most difficult to accept. Poverty occurs in some societies when one group that is in power chooses to dominate and exploit another. It is easy to condemn blatant mistreatment of a people group when it involves violence or depriving them of their human rights, but what about the exploitation of the poor for greed?

Finding Solutions

Housing alone is not the key to solving the complex issue of poverty, but it is foundational. Home ownership does offer a platform for building assets and stability and is thereby one factor in alleviating urban poverty. For example:

- Housing can be the collateral necessary for credit and the development of local and national financial institutions.
- Housing can be a catalyst for economic development by providing access to an array of construction jobs, which enables recent migrants' entrance to the economy. It also provides a stimulus to the production of construction materials, construction services, and housing related to enterprise development.
- Housing can be a stabilizing factor for individuals, families, and communities. It can also be the catalyst for social and democratic development.

These findings and Habitat for Humanity's experiences lead me to point out three critical changes that can affect poverty housing in particular:

- First, we must improve land tenure and property rights systems for the poor.
- Second, local governments must provide services and infrastructure to poor communities in informal settlements and slums.

- Third, it is critical to secure affordable urban land in appropriate settings so that organizations like Habitat for Humanity can build desperately needed, low-income housing that allows people to become healthy, contributing members of society.

We must continue to learn not only about the complex issues related to poverty around the world, but we must also be sensitive to and collaborate with people who are a part of many different cultures. We do not have all the answers for eliminating substandard housing, but we will commit our resources both to building houses and to partnering with others to find innovative solutions.

Creating Opportunities

In the United States, breaking out of poverty is difficult, but possible. The encouraging part of the economic growth of the last fifteen years has been greater overall prosperity. At the same time, the gap between the haves and have-nots has increased in many areas of the world. In South Africa, the site of one of the world's best economic success stories, the overall economy has grown, but the story is not the same for the poor. None of the wealth has benefited the bottom 50 percent of the population.

Habitat for Humanity International is a coalition partner of the ONE Campaign and a member of the campaign's governing board, which seeks to generate financial support for the world's poorest communities. The ONE Campaign promotes the idea that providing an additional 1 percent of the U.S. budget toward basic needs such as health, education, clean water, and food would transform an entire generation. According to the ONE Campaign, surveys show that Americans think more than 15 percent of the U.S. budget is currently marked for fighting AIDS and poverty around the world. It is actually less than 1 percent of the federal budget. As the campaign suggests:

> If the U.S. were to devote an additional ONE percent—one cent more for every dollar spent by the federal government—to helping the world's poorest people help themselves, America would demonstrate a commitment to the Millennium Goals, an internationally agreed upon effort to halve global poverty by 2015. ONE percent more of the U.S. federal budget would help save millions of lives. . . . If it is delivered, we would achieve 0.35% of national wealth going to Official Development Assistance—halfway to the international commitment to achieve 0.7%.[6]

It will take all of us—governments, for-profit companies, and non-profit groups to begin to address the needs of poverty housing. After nearly twenty years of increases, growth in U.S. federal housing assistance ground to a halt in the second half of the 1990s.[7] One thing we can all do to help is to be advocates to establish housing and shelter issues as a major priority of local and federal governments. Urge support for allocating more funding to the United States Agency for International Development and other agencies for programs that address affordable housing, city planning, service delivery, financing—especially microfinancing for the poor—and local economic development. We have seen evidence that by directly investing in the poor to solve problems, such as eradicating disease, people have more energy to solve their problems.

The Biblical Model

Jesus showed us the mind-set for finding solutions. In Matthew 25 he proclaimed his identification with those in need. He is disguised among the hungry and thirsty. He comes as the stranger, as the sick, as the prisoner. It is here, among these whom Jesus described as the "least of these," that Christ is present in the world.

> WE HAVE SEEN EVIDENCE THAT BY DIRECTLY INVESTING IN THE POOR TO SOLVE PROBLEMS, SUCH AS ERADICATING DISEASE, PEOPLE HAVE MORE ENERGY TO SOLVE THEIR PROBLEMS.

Serving Christ by serving others becomes a passionate and personal endeavor for followers of Jesus. It creates a willingness to put others first, to share sacrificially, and to celebrate at the success of another.

This is where Habitat for Humanity—and other ministries that seek to serve the poor—so easily connect with the faith community. Many followers of Jesus (and those of other faiths) are seeking ways in which they can help create a just world. They welcome such tangible expressions of God's love.

Seeking Justice

Whether it is providing more people with a reasonable chance to escape the cycle of poverty in the United States or a revolutionary system to claim assets and develop capital in a developing country, this idea of leveling the playing field—of giving everyone an equal opportunity—is a common understanding of justice and one that I heard from a very early age.

My grandmother, Millicent Fenwick, whom I mentioned in the introduction to this book, was involved in the fair treatment of migrant farm workers and world famine issues, long before they were trendy issues. A congresswoman from New Jersey, she also drafted the legislation that resulted in formation of the Helsinki Commission to monitor compliance with the Helsinki accord on human rights.

My mother also had a similarly strong sense of social justice. She was involved in civil rights and in prison reform, so we often talked about major social issues of the time. I think I learned from my grandmother and both my parents that justice is how people are given not a better outcome but a fair chance in society.

A Higher Standard

I think justice is a minimum standard that we should consider for the way we treat one another. We can't count on the altruism of society, so we develop judicial systems. We attempt to develop clear laws that are consistently and fairly applied and judged by a society that does not favor one group over another. This is a baseline system for how to treat others. But doing the minimum to stay legal falls short of the kind of life God calls us to, and it certainly doesn't create an image or a reality of a civil community, let alone a Christian community.

In an address to the National Prayer Breakfast in Washington, D.C., in February 2006, rock star Bono focused on

justice in his efforts to attract support for the ONE Campaign. He applauded recent U.S. contributions to fight HIV
and malaria and offered these words:

> You're good at charity. Americans, like the Irish, are
> good at it. We like to give, and we give a lot, even those
> who can't afford it.

> But justice is a higher standard. Africa makes a fool
> of our idea of justice; it makes a farce of our idea of
> equality. It mocks our pieties, it doubts our concern, it
> questions our commitment.

> Sixty-five hundred Africans are still dying every day of
> a preventable, treatable disease, for lack of drugs we can
> buy at any drug store. This is not about charity; this is
> about justice and equality.

> Because there's no way we can look at what's happen-
> ing in Africa and, if we're honest, conclude that deep
> down, we really accept that Africans are equal to us.
> Anywhere else in the world, we wouldn't accept it.
> Look at what happened in Southeast Asia with the
> tsunami—150,000 lives lost to that misnomer of all
> misnomers, "mother nature." In Africa, 150,000 lives
> are lost every month. A tsunami every month. And it's
> a completely avoidable catastrophe. . . .

> The reason I am here, and the reason I keep coming back
> to Washington, is because this is a town that is proving
> it can come together on behalf of what the scriptures call
> the least of these. This is not a Republican idea. It is not

a Democratic idea. It is not even, with all due respect, an American idea. Nor is it unique to any one faith.

"Do to others as you would have them do to you" (Luke 6:31). Jesus says that.

"Righteousness is this: that one should . . . give away wealth out of love for Him to the near of kin and the orphans and the needy and the wayfarer and the beggars and for the emancipation of the captives." The Koran says that (2.177).

"Thus sayeth the Lord: 'Bring the homeless poor into the house, when you see the naked, cover him, then your light will break out like the dawn and your recovery will speedily spring forth, then your Lord will be your rear guard.' " The Jewish scripture says that. Isaiah 58. . . .

A number of years ago, I met a wise man who changed my life. In countless ways, large and small, I was always seeking the Lord's blessing. I was saying, "You know, I have a new song, look after it. I have a family, please look after them. I have this crazy idea. . . ."

And this wise man said: stop. He said stop asking God to bless what you're doing. Get involved in what God is doing because it's already blessed. Well, God, as I said, is with the poor. That, I believe, is what God is doing. And that is what he's calling us to do.[8]

The Implications of Justice

At a basic level, justice would mean creating a fair system with equal access to opportunity. In a country as wealthy as the United States, it might also imply some minimum basic standard of living. Beyond that it gets more complicated. Does justice mandate equal outcomes? Do you legislate redistribution of wealth? Habitat's philosophy is about opportunity rather than entitlement. Most every society does some redistribution—it is just a matter of how much based on the level of taxation and the level of social welfare.

Harvard University philosopher John Rawls sparked great discussion in his work, *A Theory of Justice*, by proposing a hypothetical exercise in which people would establish a principle of fairness (distribution of income) without knowing what their place in society would be. This "veil of ignorance," he claimed, would result in agreement of fair principles, since each person might end up at the lowest point in the social strata. He said he believed that this would guarantee that any social and economic inequalities would be considered only if the lowest level members of society would profit from the arrangement. Rawls acknowledged that inequalities would exist, but since the economic progress of the least member of society—who could be anyone—would be affected by any policy, careful decisions would be made.[9]

Rawls's emphasis on fair principles for all as they would relate to any individual is not in opposition to free market society. In fact, some would argue that if we don't have free markets, people don't have a chance to gain any assets. The additional level of consideration for free markets in a Christian culture is that we address the issues of poverty and eliminate barriers to equal opportunity.

Dr. Martin Luther King Jr. often described his ideal of a just world in terms of a beloved community, where the love of God is working in the lives of all people "moving toward justice and dignity and goodwill and respect." His widow, Coretta Scott King, elaborated on that vision many years later: "In the beloved community, the values of caring and compassion will drive policy toward the world-wide elimination of poverty and hunger, racism and all forms of bigotry and violence. The beloved community is not a place, but a state of heart and mind, a spirit of hope and goodwill that transcends all boundaries and barriers and embraces all creation."[10]

> "IN THE BELOVED COMMUNITY, THE VALUES OF CARING AND COMPASSION WILL DRIVE POLICY TOWARD THE WORLD-WIDE ELIMINATION OF POVERTY AND HUNGER, RACISM AND ALL FORMS OF BIGOTRY AND VIOLENCE."

Poverty Is the Absence of Opportunity

Addressing poverty cannot simply be about philosophies and visions, say the authors of *Opportunity and Progress: A Bipartisan Platform for National Housing Policy* from the Joint Center for Housing Studies at Harvard University. If a just society seeks to ensure equal opportunity for all—including decent shelter—then certain practical steps must be taken, the authors contend:

> Opportunity is increasingly elusive . . . for the large and growing segment of our population that lacks access to a decent home and a suitable living environment. Those

who pay too much for housing have little disposable income left for education, health care, childcare, and food. Those who live in substandard housing face physical hazards, hazards that can undermine the physical and cognitive development of children. Those who reside in neighborhoods cut off from the economic mainstream live in true poverty; they lack access to opportunities that embody the promise of advancement. Without question, safe, secure, and stable homes and neighborhoods are critical to individual achievement and community vitality.

Poverty in America is unacceptable. It is not a state of mind; it is an economic and social condition that cuts people off from opportunity. It is this absence of opportunity that translates the condition of being poor into a state of poverty. As a nation, we will overcome the problem of poverty only when we recognize that it is not self-correcting.[11]

Taking Action

If poverty issues are not going to rectify themselves, then those of us who feel called to action must work diligently. Chapter 6 offers some specific ideas that you may want to consider. The authors of the Harvard study mentioned above outline twelve specific steps that they recommend in their paper on National Housing Policy. Take a look at those ideas as you consider what you can do directly and what you can do in support of affordable housing.

As you ponder, look at what Scripture says about how we should relate to one another. Followers of Jesus realize that God intended for us to live in relationship with one another and for us to care for one another, particularly the poor. First John 4:19 says that we are to love others because God first loved us. If we fight any temptation to look for minimum standards or maximum accomplishments, we can focus on a way of life that is directed by God's unconditional and immeasurable love.

The Great Commandment (Matthew 22:37-39) also helps us understand that if we adopt an everyday mind-set of thinking beyond ourselves and showing compassion for others, the results will be amazing. Walls will melt and opportunities will emerge. If we ache for all the world to live in the safe and healthy conditions of our own families (never mind anywhere near their comfort level), the just community of which Micah spoke would begin to become a reality.

Take the Challenge: Budgeting for Poverty

The United States Conference of Catholic Bishops recently studied poverty in America today. Their study from 2006 says that U.S. government calculations indicate that a family of four earning $19,307 or less a year is living in poverty. But how far does $19,307 go in America today? How do you budget? Take a look at some annual cost estimates provided by various U.S. government agencies:

Housing for basic shelter	$5,329
Utilities to keep a family of four warm and secure	$2,309

Transportation (used car, gas, oil and maintenance)	$4,920
Food (even with public assistance such as food stamps)	$4,102
Health Care (even with employer insurance)	$2,132
Child Care (with subsidies)	$2,300
	$21,092

So now you are $1,785 over budget, and you still don't have everything you need.

What do you leave out?

- Toiletries?
- School supplies?
- Shoes?
- Clothes?
- Holiday gifts?
- Education?
- Life insurance?
- Furnishings?
- Recreation?
- Cleaning supplies?
- Entertainment?
- Birthday gifts?

These are the decisions that people are forced to make every day when they live in the state of poverty. What decisions would you make? Visit www.povertyusa.org to learn more.[12]

Reflection Questions

1. What are barriers in the United States and around the world that keep people from having fair opportunities?

2. What does a justice mind-set mean in terms of how you lead your life? Does it affect your thinking about taking tax credits? About the size living space you choose? About the transportation you select?

3. What examples can you cite in your life of "doing the minimum to stay legal" in terms of living in community? In what areas is God calling you to make a change?

4. What is the role of the religious communities in helping to create a just world for men, women, and children who do not have a safe and decent place to live? What is the role of your church or community or school? What about you?

5. Name three factors that contribute to poverty in your community. What is one specific step that you or your church or your school can do to address one of those factors? What will you commit to do?

6. Regardless of your income, calculate what you would have to do without if suddenly your net pay were reduced by 25 percent. What are the first three things you would decide to do without? What expenses that you now consider "necessities" would you have to adjust? Do the same exercise for 50 percent and 75

percent. Imagine the decisions that families living in
poverty must make every day.

7. How is a consumer-driven lifestyle perceived by individuals who are struggling to survive?

PART THREE
HOUSING
AND HUMILITY

According to Christian teachers, the essential vice, the utmost evil, is Pride. Unchastity, anger, greed, drunkenness, and all that, are mere fleabites in comparison: it was through Pride that the devil became the devil. Pride leads to every other vice: it is the complete anti-God state of mind.

—*C.S. Lewis in* Mere Christianity

First Builders from Grace Community Church in Montrose, Colorado, work on a house in a tsunami-effected area of Khao Lak, southern Thailand, in April 2005.

Chapter 5
Called to Partnership

Elena Loktionova of Siberia was absolutely in an anti-God state of mind.

She learned about Habitat for Humanity on the Internet. She was very interested in the idea of partnership housing, but when she learned that Habitat for Humanity was a Christian organization, she was not happy. She let it be known in no uncertain terms that she did not want people trying to convert her.

Still curious to see some Habitat houses being built, Loktionova discovered a Global Village project in Romania and decided to join the team to work there. She did not have money for such a trip, but she was so determined to be a part of the work team that she took out a bank loan. She arrived on a plane in Romania after two and a half days on a train from Siberia to Moscow.

Loktionova spent her fortieth birthday, which she described as the most meaningful and exciting birthday of her life, building a Habitat house with an American team. When the others learned that she had borrowed the money to make the trip, they raised the money among themselves to pay off her loan. Loktionova said she was deeply touched by the whole experience.

Upon returning home, she continued her Internet conversations, but they took on a new tone. She was so affected by the spirit and behavior of her team members and her experiences that she changed her mind completely. Ultimately, she decided to become a Christian and was baptized on an Easter Sunday.

What a transformation.

> WALKING HUMBLY WITH GOD MEANS LIVING IN COMMUNION WITH GOD AND DOING GOD'S WILL. IT IS A PERSONAL ACCEPTANCE EACH DAY THAT THE WORLD IS NOT ABOUT ME.

I want to make it clear that our unique role at Habitat for Humanity is to be a witness to the love of Jesus Christ in deed, not to convert people. But it is not surprising that we see dramatic changes in the lives of people like Elena because God's love in itself is transformational.

The humility that Micah was speaking of in the passage that helped shape this book is a personal transformation before God that can empower, not limit us. Walking humbly with God means living in communion with God and doing God's will. It is a personal acceptance each day that the world is not about me.

A Gracious Community

A practical point concerning humility for Habitat for Humanity is our attitude toward our partners. For many years

Habitat for Humanity referred to those we served as "God's people in need." One home owner proclaimed in very clear terms that she might have financial challenges but that she was otherwise a strong and blessed child of God. Several staff members were forced to examine their attitudes. Had we unconsciously taken a paternal attitude that the families we served were somehow "needy people"? That home owner caused us to look carefully at ourselves.

What about you? What is your attitude about people whom you identify as members of different financial, social, or religious groups? Do you need to experience a healthy dose of humility and consider what it would be like to be part of God's gracious community where everyone experiences love and abundance equally and shares that love eagerly?

Clarence Jordan, founder of Koinonia Farms, where the concept of partnership housing had its beginnings, wrote in his inimitable style about a gracious community in his sermon titled "A Spirit of Partnership." Despite its solely male language, it is a wonderful vision:

> **WHAT ABOUT YOU? WHAT IS YOUR ATTITUDE ABOUT PEOPLE WHOM YOU IDENTIFY AS MEMBERS OF DIFFERENT FINANCIAL, SOCIAL, OR RELIGIOUS GROUPS?**

"I will shed my spirit on all mankind." A spirit of partnership. The rich man will sit down at the same table with a poor man and learn how good cornbread and collard greens are, and the poor man will find out what a T-bone steak tastes like. Neither will shiver in a drafty house, nor have to move his furniture when it rains. Both will rejoice in the robust health of their children, who are not listless from having too little nor bored

from having too much. They will discover the blessed-
ness of sharing, the warmth of compassion, the quiet
strength of humility, and the glow of gentleness, the
cleanness of honesty, the peace of justice, the ecstasy of
love. God's spirit will let a white man look into the eyes
of a black man and see his soul; it will let a black man
look into the eyes of a white man and see his soul. And
they'll both know it's the soul of a man.

God's spirit will teach an educated man and an unedu-
cated man to walk together in the cool of the evening
after a hard day's work and both will know that one
could not live without the other. One will not ask for
more than his share and the other need not accept less
than his share. Each will delight in the skills of his
brother, and neither will exploit the other's weakness.

God's spirit will call the people from the East to join
hands with the people from the West, and the people
from the North to join hands with the people from
the South and all will seek the other's good. None will
smite his brother, nor deal deceitfully. They will sing at
their labors, and be thankful for the fruits of the fields
and factories. Their soldiers will learn the arts of peace;
their strong men the ways of service. All will be spared
the degradation of making implements of war and the
agonizing shame of using them.

God's spirit will join an old man's wisdom with a young
man's strength and they will be partners for the Lord.
They will respect one another, and will be slow to take
offense and quick to forgive. They will be as father and

son. The old man will be filled with compassion and understanding, and the young man with gentleness and loving concern. They will find joy in bearing one another's burdens.

God's spirit will give eyes to mankind with which to see the glory of the Lord. God's spirit will give ears to mankind to hear the sound of his trumpet as well as his still small voice. He will dwell with us and be our God, and we shall be his people. He will wipe away our tears, dispel our doubt, remove our fears, and lead us out. He will heal the brokenhearted, open the eyes of the blind, release the captives, preach the good news to the poor, and usher in the acceptable year of the Lord. He will bulldoze the mountains and fill in the valleys, he will make the rough places smooth and the crooked ways straight. He'll stand every man on his feet so that all mankind may see his glory together.[1]

Jordan had a profound understanding of humility—of walking humbly with the God he loved. He proclaimed that we cannot have any dealings with God unless we care for one another.

Understanding Micah's Words

When we try to understand the idea of walking humbly with God in Micah 6:8, we should look carefully at the prophet. Micah spoke the word of God between 735 and 700 BCE during the reigns of kings Jotham, Ahaz, and Hezekiah, a period of upheaval and crisis. One writer states:

The reign of Ahaz brought spiritual lethargy, apostasy and hypocrisy. The people still worshiped God, but their ritual had no life-changing reality. Their treatment of fellow Israelites violated the basic tenets of the Mosaic covenant as they failed to practice justice, and their pursuit of idolatry revealed their failure to walk humbly before God.[2]

If I restated that just a bit, it might sound very familiar: The reign of consumerism brought spiritual lethargy and hypocrisy. The people still worshiped God, but their ritual had no life-changing reality. Their treatment of their neighbors violated the basic teachings of Jesus as they failed to practice justice, and their pursuit of stuff revealed their failure to walk humbly before God.

The writer who spoke of the reign of Ahaz as a time of hypocrisy also describes chapter 6 of Micah as a lawsuit brought by God against the people of Judah over the Old Testament covenant. First of all, God lays out the charges for the case in verses 3–5, tracing his acts of mercy from the time that the people were slaves in Egypt. The charges are followed by a plea from the people as to what they must do to make things right—including the possibility of sacrificing their firstborn. The verdict is based on the covenant relationship of old. Nothing has changed in the requirements of the covenant, but Judah has broken it repeatedly. Verse 8 summarizes the entire Mosaic law: We are to focus on our relationship with God and with each other.

Worship is key in that relationship because it is the outward expression of true humility toward God, of that humble trust that is essential. Worship is more about our lives and attitude than our words or song. It is our public profession that God is God and I am not God!

Living Micah's Words

Our first call is to humble ourselves before God. Our response to God's mercy in not holding us accountable for our failures should be a renewed commitment to conform our lives to Jesus' model and to play our part in bringing heaven to earth. As a leader of a church that I formerly served says, "Let what we do in here fill the streets out there."

Sometimes that total obedience leads us to places we never imagined. For the Catholic Daughters of the Americas, it was a refusal to accept the limiting definition of humility that enabled them to start an amazing partnership with Habitat for Humanity. In 1994, this group of young-at-heart women laughed at the idea of climbing ladders and building a house. However, in April of 2006, they laughed heartily as they raised the walls on their tenth Habitat for Humanity house, which they blitz framed (built the frame of the house in a week) in Brockton, Mass., in partnership with South Shore HFH.

> OUR RESPONSE TO GOD'S MERCY IN NOT HOLDING US ACCOUNTABLE FOR OUR FAILURES SHOULD BE A RENEWED COMMITMENT TO CONFORM OUR LIVES TO JESUS' MODEL AND TO PLAY OUR PART IN BRINGING HEAVEN TO EARTH.

When Rick Beech, former church relations director for Habitat for Humanity, first approached Grace Rinaldi (who served as national regent for the Catholic Daughters in 1994) with the idea of building a Habitat house, she told him that she didn't think the women could handle construction work and all that went with it.

Beech asked why not. That bothered Rinaldi for some time until she finally said, "Okay. We'll try it." The women built their first home in Oklahoma City in 1995.

When the Daughters built their second house in Albany, New York, in 1996, Bishop Howard Hubbard of the Albany Diocese said, "In twenty years as bishop, I have never seen the Catholic community come together as visibly and forcefully as in this Habitat project." Reaching out in obedience transformed not only those served, but the serving community as well.

The Catholic Daughters have since built a house every year in partnership with a different Habitat for Humanity affiliate in the United States. The model that they have followed for each house calls for the local and state organizations, called courts, in the location where the build is to take place to raise half the money for the house. The national board of the Catholic Daughters matches the other half of the cost. Then volunteers from across the country travel to the work site to work on the home.

In addition to the annual home building projects, the Catholic Daughters have partnered with Habitat for Humanity to provide funding for tsunami relief in Asia and for hurricane relief in the Gulf. They are continuing to find ways to increase their opportunities to serve more families.

Another faithful partner in our work has been Thrivent Financial for Lutherans, a fraternal benefit organization that has supported Habitat for many years. Most recently, Thrivent Financial made an investment of volunteers and $105 million to increase significantly our annual house production around the world during a four-year period. This alliance is designed to encourage new partnerships, attract volunteers, access new resources, and raise awareness for the issue of decent housing.

One of the beneficiary families of the Thrivent Financial program are Nurri and Ayalnesh Omer and their four children of Seattle, Washington. They will move from a cramped, ant-infested apartment that has a serious mold problem and will no longer have to contend with lights that don't work and appliances that are inoperable. The Omer's children will no longer live in a high-crime area where it is unsafe to play outside.

This is a situation where the entire community benefits. The Seattle community puts a high priority on preserving affordable housing and protecting the environment by keeping homes "with possibility" out of the landfill. The city donated a dilapidated house and lot to the local Habitat affiliate. The 1920s Tudor home, which had fallen into sad disrepair and was the last eyesore in a neighborhood that had totally transformed in the last few years, will be renovated to house the Omer family.

Along with a grant that covered 70 percent of construction costs, came dozens of volunteers from local Lutheran churches to work alongside the home buyers to rehabilitate their home.

We want to reach out and help even more families each year, and this can be done through such innovative alliances. One thing I especially appreciate is that our partners at Thrivent Financial are completely committed to this effort, and they see themselves as a partner and a catalyst in transforming communities.

Understanding the Mission

This attitude of humility, of putting God first, has to permeate throughout any faithful ministry. Jim Collins, author of the book *Good to Great*, has excellent advice for CEOs of successful companies who put the company before themselves. I think his words work for those of us who seek to put God's mission first as well:

There is a direct relationship between the absence of celebrity and the presence of good-to-great results. Why? First, when you have a celebrity, the company turns into "the one genius with 1,000 helpers." It creates a sense that the whole thing is really about the CEO. At a deeper level, we found that for leaders to make something great, their ambition has to be for the greatness of the work and the company, rather than for themselves. That doesn't mean that they don't have an ego. It means that at each decision point—at each of the critical junctures when Choice A would favor their ego and Choice B would favor the company and the work—time and again the good-to-great leaders pick Choice B. Celebrity CEOs, at those same decision points, are more likely to favor self and ego over company and work.[3]

This means a lot to me personally. I knew my first task at Habitat for Humanity had to be to learn as much as I could about the ministry. I had carefully crafted a plan that I thought would help me, but within a month of my accepting the position of CEO, Hurricane Katrina struck, and I was immersed immediately in a full-scale national disaster. My desire had been to visit all our area offices around the world early on, but I had to postpone some of those visits until we got our relief efforts established.

Despite the attention that the rebuilding efforts required, I was able to visit Asia, Latin America, Africa, and Europe in my first year. I very much wanted and needed to learn about the work Habitat is doing in all corners of the globe. Equally important, however, was that I learned more about the need for that work, that I encountered the destitute living conditions of families who struggle daily, no matter their location, their religion, their language, or anything else.

Only by having these firsthand experiences, I feel, could I most fully appreciate the importance of Habitat's work throughout the world. My heart broke numerous times during my travels. It grew heavy as I heard the stories of poverty living, and it grew burdened by the sight of families, children, living in conditions that no one should ever have to endure.

Yet I also encountered immense hope in the hearts of poor families, a kind spirit in their hands, with which they welcomed me so warmly into their homes and a collective resolve among Habitat staff and volunteers to transform lives by creating housing opportunities in partnership with these families. I was particularly struck by the wide range of contexts and construction styles and yet the consistency of the core approaches to partnering with families across the world.

I carried with me throughout my journeys a mixed bag of emotions. As I returned to my own home, I did so with an urgency, inspired by what I had seen and heard and learned, that we all need to do more to serve the "least of these" wherever we can in this world, buoyed by the compassion and commitment of Habitat partners everywhere.

Poverty housing impoverishes all of us. It is together that we will make a difference. Together we will transform lives in our world . . . more families, more neighborhoods and communities, each of us bringing to the table our own valuable skills, experiences, backgrounds, talents, passions, and commitment to our neighbors in need.

This concept of humbling ourselves before God is not to be equated with timidity. In fact, it requires a boldness to be justice seekers who are willing to step out in faith and perform radical acts of mercy. We will be audacious about our goal of

THIS CONCEPT OF HUMBLING OURSELVES BEFORE GOD IS NOT TO BE EQUATED WITH TIMIDITY. IN FACT, IT REQUIRES A BOLDNESS TO BE JUSTICE SEEKERS WHO ARE WILLING TO STEP OUT IN FAITH AND PERFORM RADICAL ACTS OF MERCY.

eliminating poverty housing but humble about our role in achieving that goal. Walking humbly with God enables us to be a part of realizing God's kingdom here on earth through building relationships with God and with one another.

Matthew Maury, HFHI area vice president in Africa and the Middle East, said, "Habitat for Humanity's ministry is all about people. It is about people whose lives are being transformed. Some of the greatest impact of the kingdom-building work of HFH has been seen not just in the lives of the communities in which we work but also in the lives of people who choose to partner with families in need of decent shelter. I have worked alongside staff and volunteers who, because of their work with HFH, have come to know the freedom and love of Christ in much deeper ways."

Experiencing the kingdom happens not only in the building of relationships that comes in building houses with others but also in the transformational moments when we see glimpses of the life that God intends for us. Paul Wood, rural church relations specialist for HFHI, explains. "The truly rich are those who know that economic wealth can be an impediment to identifying with and walking with those locked in loneliness and despair through poverty. I have found that there are many such rich people in congregations throughout North America. Perhaps Habitat puts a crack in the wall that economic wealth and security builds. In this sense, Habitat can be the servant of the church that it desires to be. Becoming a vehicle for the church to be involved with people outside their group, whatever that group may be, is a significant part of our work."

Erasing Lines of Status and Presumption

First Presbyterian Church in Annapolis, Maryland, illustrates well this idea of moving the church out into the community. Everything was in place to complete a house in partnership with Arundel HFH, but then the walls fell down! Former pastor Timothy J. Havlicheck explained:

> How could this have happened? It was not for lack of planning. For months, First Presbyterian had the dream of fully sponsoring the building of a house for Habitat and outlined to the minute detail the path toward making that dream a reality. Everything was set forth in specifics, and the construction was accomplished ahead of schedule.
>
> It was not for lack of resources. Generous contributions poured in and volunteers stepped forward to offer their skills and gifts in both hammering nails and providing the support of prayers and meals; people surprised one another with their hidden talents. Anxieties quickly disappeared into the awe of church mobilization.
>
> And it was not for the lack of commitment. The congregation truly wanted to make the project happen, to make a tangible difference for one family's life, and thereby declare to a whole city what can happen when

people work together for good. Our hearts led us to proclaim in deed the love of Christ.

But as the house went up, the "walls" unexpectedly came down. Member worked side-by-side with member with never a thought as to differing political views or theological perspectives. Worship and work surrounding the project was shared quite naturally with African-American brothers and sisters from our [home owner] family's home church. Neighborhood families and former Habitat house recipients whom we barely knew quickly became partners and friends. Those who thought they did not have the time or ability to make a difference found themselves immersed in making God's kingdom appear on earth.

Serving Together

Habitat for Humanity is based on such biblical principles as sharing our resources, trusting in God, and tithing. Habitat for Humanity groups around the world are urged to donate 10 percent of the money they raise locally to send to another area of the world to help build more houses. This continuous cycle of giving is one of the foundations that connects us to the church.

Habitat projects have also been successful in bringing together different groups within the church. Baptists have worked with Catholics, and Presbyterians have joined with Lutherans and United Methodists to build homes. Other unlikely partners have united in the name of Habitat for Humanity as well: Democrats have partnered with Republicans, folks from the west side of town have crossed the river to work in the neighborhoods on the east side, and CEOs have painted walls alongside folks who don't have offices on the executive floors. In the United States we often refer to this coming together for the common purpose of building a home as "the theology of the hammer."

International projects have led to partnerships that enabled people to learn about other cultures and, in some cases, develop long-lasting friendships. Churches in the United States and Canada, for example, worked together for a number of years on building projects in El Salvador before a five-year, 500-house, church-sponsored campaign was developed. Volunteers told of how they traveled hundreds of miles expecting to help others but returned as the ones who were blessed. One home owner offered words of thanks that she finally had a home large enough to host a Bible study. So when we talk of transformational ministry, we are talking not only of integrating housing and a variety of ministries into communities that demonstrate great need. We are also recognizing how God works in the lives of many people to deepen their faith and understanding of the amazing love of Jesus Christ.

We also partner with people of other faiths. Many houses have been built by Jewish congregations, Muslim groups, B'hai partners, and others. We are proudly a Christian ministry that welcomes people of all faiths and no faith to join us in our work. Our role of transformation is helping people view themselves as citizens of the

> WHEN WE TALK OF TRANSFORMATIONAL MINISTRY, WE ARE TALKING NOT ONLY OF INTEGRATING HOUSING AND A VARIETY OF MINISTRIES INTO COMMUNITIES THAT DEMONSTRATE GREAT NEED. WE ARE ALSO RECOGNIZING HOW GOD WORKS IN THE LIVES OF MANY PEOPLE.

world and to help them experience what authentic community can be.

My invitation to anyone is, "We would love to have you join us, and we are going to partner with you in a way that is respectful of who you are."

More than Houses

Long-term projects, such as the El Salvador campaign, are part of a program known as Global Church Partnerships, which focuses on a holistic approach to ministry. It is important to let churches and other communities set the vision for how they want to address social and spiritual issues and for how Habitat can be involved as a facilitator for building something new.

When organizers start to design the project, they talk to the churches about the kind of outreach they provide or would like to provide in the community. That might be food, supplies for vacation Bible school, scholarships for school, or other services. Many times building houses with Habitat for Humanity is just one of the ministries being organized by the churches and the local communities. Teams from churches going to other countries may commit to help build a certain number of houses over a multiyear period. We try to do community transformation the way it should be done, with the community organizing and taking charge to transform their current situation.

Partners with Similar Goals

Our work in the Gulf following hurricanes Katrina and Rita has led us to partner with like-minded organizations to help with the enormous tasks of rebuilding in areas devastated by the storms. We are working with the Local Initiatives Support Corporation and the Enterprise organization to help local community development groups in the region.

Habitat for Humanity as a Catalyst

In 2005, the international board of directors for Habitat for Humanity was asked to envision the ministry in 2111. One of the distinctive changes that board members said they would like to see was for Habitat to recast itself in a slightly humbler way, one in which it is more like a critical spoke and less like the hub. Their vision is one in which Habitat sees itself as one of the many players seeking to end poverty housing, and one in which HFH might serve as catalyst and mobilizer rather than simply as a housing provider. In the board's vision, partnership will begin to extend beyond partnerships with donors, volunteers, and home buyers and will extend to other international service organizations. Their hypothesis is that perhaps together, more can be done. Perhaps together, we can, in fact, realize our ultimate goal: a world without poverty housing. In a word, their vision for HFH is that of a catalyst.

How about you? I have told numerous stories about what a difference one person can make when he or she feels called to action. How are you going to make a difference? Look at the ideas in chapter 6 and consider what you might do.

Questions for Reflection

1. How do you now understand the concept of walking humbly with God?

2. How do you respond to Clarence Jordan's idea that we cannot have any dealings with God unless we care for one another the way he described in "A Spirit of Partnership" on page 77?

3. Does the idea of total obedience seem freeing or constraining? Explain and give examples.

4. When have you been humbled by the actions of God in a specific situation that were beyond your ability to imagine?

5. How is building houses (or serving in other ways) a way to help build the kingdom of God?

6. What is one thing you will commit to do within the next month to fill the streets with the love that God has shown to you?

Chapter 6
What Is Your Call?

In 1997, when Jean and Pat Smith were making plans to celebrate their fiftieth birthdays, they considered taking a vacation to an exotic location. Instead, they opted for a volunteer mission experience. What started as a two-week trip changed their lives, revitalized a community of Habitat for Humanity home owners in Ghana, and turned into a major mission effort for the Roman Catholic Cathedral of Christ the King in Lexington, Kentucky.

"The idea of a trip to Africa had intrigued me since I was a child," said Pat. "After a few conversations, Jean also became excited about the possibility of an African adventure." So the couple joined a Habitat Global Village work team. "We had never been to a Third World country and really didn't know what we were getting into at the time."

During their two-week stay in the rural bush village of Assasan, the Smiths learned that the Catholic church there had fallen into such disrepair that it had to be torn down several years earlier. Many of the Habitat home owners in the community were Catholic but had no place to worship.

After returning home, Pat said the couple continued to think about their friends in Assasan. "Walking into our cathedral didn't seem right, knowing they had no church in which to worship," said Pat. So in December of 1997, the Smiths solicited support from their congregation to fund construction of a new church in Assasan. They raised more than $50,000 in less than two months. Elementary children alone collected more than $6,000 in coins for the project.

Villagers in Assasan had estimated it would take up to twenty-five years to build their church, but with the help of returning teams from Christ the King, the structure was ready in less than fourteen months. "Christ the King Church in Assasan stands as proof that with dedication and passion, anything is possible," said Pat.

Pat was an active leader in the Habitat for Humanity affiliate in Lexington and was a key figure in Habitat's recent disaster relief efforts in Asia and the Gulf. Following the tsunami in December of 2004, he was one of the first to respond with a Habitat team traveling to Sri Lanka. Afterward, he described the absolute devastation everywhere.

"We often met people wanting to tell their stories, and they are hard to listen to," he said. "I walked over to the shore to take a picture of a wrecked fishing boat. In the middle of the field, near a tent city, were a man, wife, and child sitting under a tree. He motioned for me to come, and I did. The wife was holding a 10 x 12 inch framed picture of their daughter. She was very beautiful and I guess about fourteen. The mother was crying and said simply, 'tsunami, tsunami.' There was nothing I could say except, 'I'm sorry.'"

Pat was named Habitat for Humanity International's volunteer of the year in 2003 and was elected to the HFHI board of directors in 2005.

Again, Pat was eager to do the physical work of helping families get back in their homes following the destruction of the hurricanes in the Gulf. He was on his way to join a construction team in Gulfport, Mississippi, when he was killed in a plane crash in August of 2006.

Pat Smith was a great friend to Habitat for Humanity. A passionate spirit and infinite energy were ignited in one man to do so many great things. Pat motivated others to try something new. He made a difference in the lives of people around the world. What about you? What difference can you make? What are you willing to try that you have never done before?

Self-Assessment

In Part One of this book we talked about going out of our way to extend acts of mercy and compassion. Those acts often take us out of our daily routine and require some effort on our part. Think back on the last month or so. Have you done anything that you would consider an act of mercy? How willing are you to be late for an appointment or to approach a stranger or to deprive yourself to do something extraordinary for someone who obviously needs assistance? What keeps you from such actions?

In Part Two, we talked about justice and how it is often equated with fairness—as the minimum standard for the way we treat one another. Yet we continued to say that doing the minimum falls short of the kind of life to which

HAVE YOU DONE ANYTHING THAT YOU WOULD CONSIDER AN ACT OF MERCY? HOW WILLING ARE YOU TO BE LATE FOR AN APPOINTMENT OR TO APPROACH A STRANGER OR TO DEPRIVE YOURSELF TO DO SOMETHING EXTRAORDINARY FOR SOMEONE WHO OBVIOUSLY NEEDS ASSISTANCE? WHAT KEEPS YOU FROM SUCH ACTIONS?

God calls us. How about you? What does the idea of justice mean in your life? Where do issues of justice confront you? Consider how God's Word through the prophet Micah calls you to do justice.

Finally, in Part Three we talked about humility in the sense of living in communion with God to do God's will. When we present ourselves totally before God, a transformation takes place. What specific events in your life occurred because you were willing to be completely obedient to God?

Micah says that God requires these three things: that we act justly, love mercy, and walk humbly with God. Our trust in a loving God reminds us that Micah's requirements are not constraints but rather the map for us to better understand how God intends for us to live an abundant life. What are some spiritual practices that allow you to follow these three requirements more faithfully?

Following Your Passion

You cannot ignore the issues that pull on your heart when God is calling you to respond to a particular need. You may be drawn to help children (or adults) learn to read. If so, find out about literacy programs in your community or volunteer at your neighborhood school. If the idea of children who are hungry or individuals who lack basic medical care are stirring in your soul, then seek out hunger programs or medical mission teams that you can support. Follow your passion and then be passionate about following God's call. If affordable housing is tugging at your heart, the suggestions in the rest of this chapter can help you decide what you can do to help.

> OUR TRUST IN A LOVING GOD REMINDS US THAT MICAH'S REQUIREMENTS ARE NOT CONSTRAINTS BUT RATHER THE MAP FOR US TO BETTER UNDERSTAND HOW GOD INTENDS FOR US TO LIVE AN ABUNDANT LIFE.

Getting Involved with Housing Issues

Affordable housing is a complex issue that is going to require fresh thinking and cooperation on a global scale. In your work, through your church, as a volunteer, through political advocacy, or through financial investments, you may be able to help address some of the issues that contribute to growing poverty issues around the world. You can start out taking small steps, or you may be fired up to make things happen on a larger scale. Seek God's guidance as you offer yourself as the hands and feet of Jesus.

Opportunities for Individuals to Partner with Habitat for Humanity

All of Habitat for Humanity's work is done through local groups called affiliates. Go to our Web site (www.habitat. org), and on the home page you will find a link called "Local

Affiliates." That will take you to a page that will help you find the name and contact information for the affiliate nearest you. You can also find links to local Web sites for many affiliates.

Get in touch with the local Habitat for Humanity leaders and ask about some of the possibilities listed below. Get your entire office or student group or church involved.

- **Pray.** Habitat for Humanity is dependent upon the prayer support of people around the world. Pray for those in need of housing and for those who give of their time and resources, and pray that God will continue to bless this ministry.
- **Volunteer** and recruit others to volunteer regularly with your local affiliate. Many affiliates work on Saturdays. Some have additional workdays during the week.
- **Serve on a committee.** Operating a Habitat for Humanity affiliate requires many people with a variety of skills. Family Selection, Family Nurture, Publicity, Land Acquisition, and Church Relations are just a few of the committees that need volunteers.
- **Prepare and serve meals.** What a blessing it is to construction volunteers when others provide lunches, drinks, snacks, and even cold water or hot coffee, depending on the weather.
- **Donate.** Consider the cost of the roof for your own house. The price of an entire home in Brazil is $4,000. Before anyone can swing a hammer or begin stacking bricks, materials must be purchased. Building houses costs money.
- **Join a Global Village team.** Work alongside people in a host community in another culture. By working

together with a traveling team, you can help build a true global village of love, homes, communities, and hope!

Opportunities for Churches and Other Groups to Partner with Habitat for Humanity

- **Participate in the Day of Prayer.** Each year on the third Sunday in September, Habitat for Humanity observes the International Day of Prayer and Action for Human Habitat. Churches around the world are urged to pray for those in need of shelter and are encouraged to pray that God will touch the hearts of people to respond to that need.
- **Support Habitat for Humanity financially.** Make a donation, organize a fund-raising event, take up a special collection, or put Habitat for Humanity in the church budget.
- **Form a Global Church Partnership team.** Partner with churches in other parts of the world to develop ongoing relationships to build houses and provide other ministries to transform communities.
- **Participate in a special campaign.** Be a partner in a Women Build, Youth United, Building on Faith project (Habitat's focus on church partners), or an Apostles Build, where twelve churches join together to fund and build a Habitat for Humanity house.
- **Partner with Habitat to fund and build one or more houses.** Commit to raise the funds and provide the volunteers needed to build one or more houses. The Habitat affiliate will provide the lot, select the family,

take care of all the legal work, and provide construction supervision.
- **Think big.** In partnership with larger churches, denominational groups, or organizations, work with a local affiliate to revitalize a neighborhood or to build a number of houses in another country where houses cost less.

Check out our Web site, www.habitat.org, for more information.

Housing Advocacy Opportunities

Habitat for Humanity has always had a two-pronged goal—to raise awareness of the problem of poverty housing and to be a part of the solution. Our goal is to make it religiously and politically unacceptable for anyone to live without decent, affordable housing. A major call of the Old and New Testaments is ministry with and for the poor. Thus, partner churches and other groups can play a key role in this consciousness-raising effort. Churches can provide the faith roots to motivate new calls to action. Churches and other religious groups can make clear God's biblical call to end poverty and can share the imperative for decent housing. You can:

- lead in the identification and elimination of the root causes of poverty housing.
- mobilize community leaders to help shape local, state, and national public policy toward eliminating poverty and poverty housing.
- lead in the formation of local partnerships toward transforming communities whose goals are that all

persons have the opportunity to have a decent place to live, whether through home ownership, public rental, private rental, or other means.

- be instrumental in influencing faith groups and other organizations on college and university campuses and in high school settings toward understanding and responding to the biblical call to end poverty and poverty housing in the world.
- work through Habitat campus chapters as well as directly with faith groups on campuses.
- influence denominations and other national and international bodies to work for the elimination of substandard housing.
- do research and hold informational meetings.
- communicate with legislators.
- write articles describing your experiences for local newspapers and church/campus/community publications.
- work with denominational or church networks to recruit other churches. Churches understand the power of telling the story. Help volunteers find opportunities to give their witness so they might change laws, opinions, hearts, and minds.

Housing as a National Priority

An excellent resource for advocacy information is the paper entitled *Opportunity and Progress: A Bipartisan Platform for National Housing Policy* from the Joint Center for Housing Studies at Harvard University. The authors of the study offer the twelve recommendations that follow to reassert housing as a national priority. The suggestions include continuation of some policies that are in place and expansion of others to include new thinking and cooperation on federal and local levels and with the private sector.

"The mission of government—and indeed a central public value of our society—is to steer our national engines of liberty and enterprise so that they create opportunities for self-improvement for all Americans and create choices about the quality of our lives," say the authors. "We must recognize that housing is part of a larger public policy environment that includes education, wages and incomes and health security. Decent housing is a precursor to learning, earning and health."[1]

Their policy recommendations include:

1. End chronic homelessness by funding housing and services to people who face chronic challenges.
2. Redirect public housing funding streams.
3. Protect and expand the Housing Choice Voucher program.
4. Establish a national housing trust fund to support the production, preservation, and rehabilitation of 1.5 million affordable housing units over the next ten years.
5. Eliminate regulatory barriers to the production of workforce housing.
6. Enact a federal home ownership tax credit.
7. Create incentives for employers to provide housing assistance.
8. Preserve the affordability of privately owned multi-family rental housing.
9. Redefine the affordable housing mission for the government-sponsored enterprises. (Fannie Mae, Freddie Mac, and Federal Home Loan Banks).

10. Prohibit predatory lending.
11. Institute university-based programs to train the nation's housing professionals.
12. Vigorously enforce the nation's Fair Housing and Fair Lending laws

For more information go to www.jchs.harvard.edu.

Sarath Tikiribandara, a Save & Build home owner, with his daughter near their Habitat house in Adiranigama Village, Sri Lanka.

What You Need to Know about Habitat for Humanity

We believe in the promises of Scripture that God has blessed this ministry and will continue to bless those who serve with a humble spirit. As a Christian ministry, we follow the example of Jesus to welcome all those who will join us in our work.

Habitat groups, called affiliates, work locally in communities around the world to select and support home owners, organize volunteers, and coordinate house building. Home owners are selected based on their need for housing, their ability to repay their mortgage, and their willingness to work in partnership with Habitat.

Habitat for Humanity helps families who might not ordinarily qualify for conventional loans to become home owners. Individuals, churches, businesses, civic groups, and others who provide vital financial support and volunteer labor make it possible to sell Habitat houses through no-profit mortgages. Habitat home owners make downpayments and perform sweat-equity hours by helping to build their homes and the homes of others. At closing, they assume the mortgages on the homes.

As we go about our work around the world each day, we seek to keep our mission before us. In all that we do in pursuing the mission of Habitat for Humanity, we pledge to:

1. **Demonstrate the love and teachings of Jesus Christ.** We will act in all ways in accord with the belief that God's love and grace abound for all; that every human life is priceless; that we must never exploit another for our own profit; that Christ can multiply the miniscule to accomplish the magnificent; and that we are to act as faithful stewards of the resources we receive.

2. **Advocate on behalf of those in need of decent shelter.** We commit, as an integral part of our work, to communicating the needs of all people for safe and decent shelter, thereby engaging in deliberate efforts to leverage change within society to eliminate restraints that contribute to poverty and poverty housing.

3. **Focus on shelter by building and renovating simple, decent, affordable houses.**
   We have chosen, as our means of manifesting God's love, to build adequate and durable homes with those in need of shelter, carrying out the belief that safe and affordable housing is a basic human right and a fundamental component of dignity and long-term well-being for every person on earth.

4. **Engage broad community through inclusive leadership and diverse partnerships.**
   We will work in people-to-people partnership. Following Christ's example, we believe that everyone—

regardless of race, nationality, religion, or socioeconomic status—can work together for the good of all; that everyone can unite behind serving those in need within a human community; and that everyone has something to contribute to the work of building houses and hope.

5. **Promote dignity through full partnership with Habitat home owners and future home partners.**
   We put into practice the belief that healthy self-regard—and the benefits that derive from that sense of worth—is promoted not simply by living in an adequate house, but by fully contributing to the process of acquiring that house and by the opportunity to help others also acquire adequate shelter. Promoting dignity also refers to the nondiscriminatory selection of all home partners based on need and willingness to partner.

6. **Promote transformational and sustainable community development.**
   We view our work as successful when it promotes holistic and lasting positive change within a community; when it helps empower those who have been powerless; when it is based on mutual trust and fully shared accomplishment; when it promotes improved relationships among all peoples; when its goal is local, community leadership for ongoing work; and when it demonstrates respectful stewardship of all human, economic, and natural resources.

A Habitat home owner receives the key to a brand new home.

Notes

Chapter 3

1. *The State of the Nation's Housing 2006* (Cambridge: Joint Center for Housing Studies of Harvard University, 2006), 25.

2. The National Low Income Housing Coalition, "NLIHC Releases 2005 Housing Affordability Report," Washington, D.C. The report calculates the number of full-time minimum wage earners a household needs to afford the Fair Market Rent as calculated by HUD in any area of the country.

3. *Effects of Improved Housing on Illness in Children under Five Years Old in Northern Malawi: Cross-Sectional Study*, www.habitat.org/hfhu/programs/research/malawipaper. aspx. No date given.

4. Ani de la Quintano and Lisa A. Warner, *More than Houses: The Impact of Housing on the Lives of Partner Families*

(Costa Rica: Department of Communications and Community Mobilization, Habitat for Humanity Area Office in Latin America and Caribbean, 2005), 17, 18, 24.

5. Henry G. Cisneros, Jack F. Kemp, Nicolas P. Retsinas, and Kent W. Colton, *Opportunity and Progress: A Bipartisan Platform for National Housing Policy* (Cambridge: Joint Center for Housing Studies of Harvard University, 2006), 4.

Chapter 4

1. Hernando DeSoto, "Capitalism and the Road to Prosperity," *Commanding Heights*, PBS, March 30–31, 2001. http://www.pbs.org/wgbh/commandingheights/shared/minitextlo/int_hernandodesoto.html.

2. Matt Moffett, "Barrio Study Links Land Ownership to a Better Life," *Wall Street Journal*, November 9, 2005, A1.

3 *International Workshop on Education and Poverty Eradication, Kampala, Uganda, 30 July to 3 August 2001*, The United Nations Educational, Scientific and Cultural Organization, http:www.unesco.org/education/poverty/news.shtml.

4 Miloon Kothari, *Economic, Social and Cultural Rights: Women and Adequate Housing* (United Nations Commission on Human Rights: 2005) 2, 15, 17, 19.

5. Dr. Sandra Joireman, "The Importance of Securing Property Rights in Africa," *The Forum*, Habitat for Humanity International (2006). http://partnernet.habitat.org/intradoc/groups/hfhi/documents/periodicals/1theimpo.hcsp.

6. ONE: The Campaign to Make Poverty History, www.one.org/About.html.

7. *The State of the Nation's Housing, 2005* (Cambridge: Joint Center for Housing Studies of Harvard University, 2006), 29.

8. Bono, "Bono's Best Sermon Yet: Remarks at the National Prayer Breakfast," February 2, 2006, http://www.data.org/archives/000774.php.

9. John Rawls, *A Theory of Justice* (Cambridge: Belknap Press, 1971).

10. Jerry Martin, "King Shares Hope for Beloved Community," *Flyer News: University of Dayton's Independent Student Newspaper* 52, no. 33 (March 8, 2005), http://www.flyernews.com/article.php?section=News&volume=52&issue=33&artnum=02.

11. *Opportunity and Progress: A Bipartisan Platform for National Housing Policy* (Joint Center for Housing Studies of Harvard University, Cambridge: 2004), 1, 2.

12. "Budgeting for Poverty," United States Conference of Catholic Bishops, Washington, D.C. Used with permission. See also www.povertyusa.org.

Chapter 5

1. Clarence Jordan, *The Substance of Faith and Other Cotton Patch Sermons* (Eugene, Ore: Wipf & Stock, 2005), 177–79. Permission is granted by Koinonia Partners and the Jordan family.

2. Ralph L. Smith, *Word Biblical Commentary Vol. 32: Micah–Malachi* (Waco, Texas: Word Books, 1984).

3. Jim Collins, "Good to Great," *Fast Company*, October 2001, 90, http://pf.fastcompany.com/magazine/51/goodto-great.html.

Chapter 6

1. Henry G. Cisneros, Jack F. Kemp, Nicolas P. Retsinas, and Kent W. Colton, *Opportunity and Progress, A Bipartisan Platform for National Housing Policy* (Cambridge: Joint Center for Housing Studies of Harvard University, 2004), 8. Authors of this important paper bring experience and dedication to their work:

- Henry G. Cisneros is former U.S. HUD secretary and chair of American CityVista, a homebuilding enterprise focused on "villages within the city" in the central neighborhoods of metropolitan areas.
- Jack F. Kemp is also a former HUD secretary and co-director of Empower America, a public policy and advocacy organization.
- Nicolas P. Retsinas is director of Harvard University's Joint Center for Housing Studies and a lecturer in housing studies.
- Kent W. Colton, Ph.D., is president of K. Colton LLC and a senior scholar at Harvard University's Joint Center for Housing Studies.